THE PRINCIPLES OF WAR

DR. RICK JOYNER &
LTG (R) W.G. "JERRY" BOYKIN

MorningStar Publications
www.MorningStarMinistries.org

The Principles of War
By Dr. Rick Joyner & LTG (R) W.G. "Jerry" Boykin

©2021 1st Printing

MorningStar Ministries, Fort Mill, SC. All rights reserved.

**Distributed by MorningStar Publications, Inc.,
a division of MorningStar Fellowship Church
375 Star Light Drive, Fort Mill, SC 29715**

**www.MorningStarMinistries.org
1-800-542-0278**

Unless otherwise indicated, Scripture quotations are taken from the New American Standard Version. Copyright © 1995 by Thomas Nelson, Inc. Used by permission. All rights reserved.

No part of this book may be reproduced or transmitted in any form or by any means, electronic, or mechanical, including photocopying, recording, or by any information storage and retrieval system, without written permission from the author.

Cover and layout design: Carlie McKinley

ISBN: 978-1-60708-668-0
For a free catalog of MorningStar Resources, please call 1-800-542-0278

TABLE OF CONTENTS

Chapter 1

Introduction to The Principles of War

RJ: This work takes the principles of war and military strategy and adopts them so they can be applied to almost any business venture, enterprise, mission, or sport. These military principles were developed from thousands of years of experience in war—successes and failures—and provide an indispensable resource that every new warrior can learn from in just a few hours of study. The same is true for those who apply them to any other venture. Consequently, those who know and apply these principles will have a major advantage over those who do not.

As military studies apply these principles to military uses, this work, after explaining their military application, applies this amazing wisdom to all other types of ventures. They can be a major help in defining overall purpose, goals, and simplifying strategy.

This work is based loosely on the essay, "Principles of War," which was expanded into the book *On War* by Carl von Clausewitz. These were written following the Napoleonic wars which dominated Europe until 1814. As was common was common during these times of often shifting alliances, Clausewitz fought both for Napoleon and at times against him. There may not have been a better time in history for defining the principles of war than this period, and Clausewitz was an astute observer and learner. His works are classics studied by military leaders around the world to this day.

It seems Clausewitz only wrote one version of *Principles of War*, but today there are quite a few different works attributed to him by the same title. During the time Gen. Boykin and I were contemplating this work based on Clausewitz's eleven principles, I (RJ) was at the Waterloo Battlefield Park outside of Brussels and found a French volume of Clausewitz's work in the bookstore titled *The Twelve Principles of War*. I have since seen volumes that addressed nine and ten principles of war, all claiming to be Clausewitz's original work. What should we do with this seeming confusion? Nothing. Use them all!

We may be convinced the original addressed eleven principles. However, there were subprinciples Clausewitz addressed under one of eleven that could be elevated to a main principle. Some authors elevated one or more subprinciples. Others did not. But all are important and useful. So, we have covered them all, even the subcategories.

This work began when Lt. Gen. (Ret.) Jerry Boykin and I taught these principles together. General Boykin is one of the remarkable military leaders of recent times. He is a founding member of the U.S. Army's Delta Force. He later commanded Delta in some of its most important battles, including the Panama invasion and the Battle of Mogadishu immortalized by the book and movie *Black Hawk Down*. He then rose to command all U.S. Army Special Forces, and after two years overseeing covert operations at the CIA, he became Deputy Secretary of Defense for Intelligence. This gives him a unique and vast experience for understanding our times.

When Gen. Boykin and I taught these principles, he would explain each one and its military application, then I would share how they could be applied to business, politics, missions, sports, or just about any endeavor. Every time we taught this, we would get requests to put this material in a book, which you now have in your hands.

Though I had one tour of duty in the U.S. Navy, most of my life has been in leadership at various levels. However, I have studied military history for over fifty years. I did this as a student of leadership because military history has some of the most important and insightful examples of leadership, as do the principles of war.

I applied some of these principles when I started an aviation business. It grew into one of the most diverse and busiest in the nation in just three years. After this, I founded a Christian publishing organization, and in less than two years our works reached the top of bestseller lists and were being distributed around the world. Both organizations grew well beyond the rate that would destroy most organizations, which militaries must face almost every time war breaks out. Many principles I learned by studying military leadership helped me navigate the many crises that came with fast growth.

The aviation business became diverse as we grew. I leased and managed the busiest airport in our state. We built one of the largest general aviation aircraft maintenance operations in the country, had aircraft sales, a flight school, and even sold aircraft insurance. We also became what an FAA examiner said was perhaps the busiest on-demand air charter service in the country.

When I left the aviation business to start writing and publishing books, my wife, Julie, and I were basically the entire staff. Quickly we had international bestsellers, some of which were translated into fifty or more languages. As we became known around the world, we added missions, schools, a fellowship of churches and ministries, music recording and distribution, television production, and purchased the largest hotel and conference center in our state for hosting conferences. As of this writing, we continue to expand operations. The ability to build and oversee such a multi-faceted and fast-growing organization I attribute to what I gleaned from constantly studying leadership, especially military leadership, and especially the principles of war.

That this work is based on principles of war is one of the factors that makes it timely. Life on this planet has always been a struggle but we are obviously in a time of increasing conflict. Growing a business can be as much about warfare as the great military campaigns of history—it is just warfare in a different form. The same principles that generals apply in military campaigns can help you with your advertising strategy and ability to increase market share. They can also help a coach build a championship team.

Consider that when Moses led Israel out of Egypt, it says they were "a great mixed multitude," which probably could have been translated "a mob." By the time they reached the Red Sea, it says they were marching in "martial array" (military order). The Lord repeatedly said in Scripture that He is a warrior. We must have military demeanor and discipline if we are going to follow Him.

Consider that Jesus told the Roman centurion that He had not found such faith in anyone in Israel. This centurion attributed his faith in Jesus to understanding military authority. Jesus did not refute this.

The first Gentile chosen by the Holy Spirit to receive the gospel was another centurion. Why? There is a connection between those with military discipline, demeanor, and understanding and usefulness to the Lord. The Lord even referred to Himself as "Captain of the hosts of the Lord," which means Captain of the Armies of the Lord.

In America, we have been embroiled in almost continuous wars for the last twenty years, yet only about 1% of the population has military experience. How can the other 99% get this experience that translates into character, demeanor, and leadership, which can help us become more effective? By learning to apply these principles of war to every endeavor.

This does not mean we should all be saluting, calling superiors "sir," or even be disciplined for dereliction of duty or disobeying orders. Rather factors like basic organization, the ability to see our objectives clearly, and developing plans for attaining them could all be a major help to any organization.

In a culture that is now falling into increasing lawlessness, chaos, and confusion, having some structure and seriousness about us should become increasingly appealing to nearly everyone. We don't want to quickly replace the lack of discipline now found in most organizations with a Gestapo, but we can change this increasingly chaotic culture into a far more disciplined and focused one if we use wisdom.

During World War II, the American population was highly mobilized, structured, and had a basic military demeanor throughout the country. Everyone learned not to be late for work or become slack in their work, or someone else would be given their job. It had to be that way; we were at war. We are at war now against enemies both foreign and domestic. Our Constitutional Republic is being held together by a thread. To survive these times, and more importantly, to turn them into a great opportunity we must quickly recover the type of serious demeanor that wars require.

During World War II, those who were fighting battles in the military thought they were so far behind in their civilian job skills and professions they would never have a chance to catch up after the war. Many thought it would be difficult to even get a job when they returned home. For reasons they did not perceive but we now understand, they could not have been more wrong.

The returning veterans may have been behind in skills, knowledge, and experience, but they had gained other things far more valuable. Like leadership, how to endure and fight against seemingly impossible odds, and basic resourcefulness to leap over nearly all who were ahead of them in the workforce. They had experience dealing with crises far more serious than those found in any civilian job, so they did not panic. Instead, they were disciplined, wise, and resourceful in crises. And soon the veterans had risen to the top in nearly every field and industry.

The future belongs to the disciplined, wise, and resourceful, who combine these attributes with courage to stand firmly against seemingly impossible odds. Understanding and applying these principles of war can help us do this.

The real hero is the man who fights even though he is scared. Some men get over their fright in a minute under fire. For some, it takes an hour. For some it takes days. But a real man will never let his fear of death overpower his honor, his sense of duty to his country and his innate manhood.

– Gen. George S. Patton (*Speeches That Changed the World,* pages 112-114)

Chapter 2

Objective

RJ: The first step in any operation is to define the objective. The success of the operation can be determined by how clear the objective is and how focused on it we remain. As Peter Lord once said, "The main thing is to keep the main thing the main thing." The objective is the "main thing."

The objective must be identifiable and understandable to those who must execute it. This is especially important in combat because the "fog of war" is almost always present in battle. This "fog" is the result of constant unanticipated changing situations and the fact that there are no perfect, failsafe plans. We do the best we can with what we know and try to prepare for the unexpected. Knowing our objective and remaining focused on it helps us stay on point and adjust as necessary.

This is crucial because many battles on the verge of victory were turned into defeats because secondary opportunities sidetracked the forces from their objective. Consequently, opportunities can arise that are far more valuable than the original objective. Thus, the decision to change an objective for any reason should always remain with the commander who then makes this adjustment clear to the forces.

One of the greatest military examples of keeping the objective in focus comes from the American Civil War. After General Ulysses S. Grant had taken command of all Union Armies, he faced Confederate General Robert E. Lee. Grant's army was quickly and badly beaten in his first engagement against Lee's Confederates. Grant's commanders started calling for a hasty retreat to Washington, so Lee could not cut off their escape. Grant replied their objective was not Washington but Richmond, the Confederate capital.

The next morning, as General Lee observed Grant's forces marching south toward Richmond instead of retreating to Washington, he told his staff the war was lost. The Union finally had a leader who would not be deterred from his objective. Success almost always requires such focus and resolve.

In military operations, there are two basic ways to define the objective: the mission and the commander's intent. Any soldier in command must constantly reflect on the objective and actions of the combatants both for and against. The method for achieving the objective may change when conditions change, but the objective itself should not be changed except by the commander.

Mission Creep

When the objective is not clear it can be misunderstood, making focus on it difficult or lost. That is when "mission creep" occurs. The executing unit begins to take on new tasks that divert it from its original objective. Though this may accomplish some things, those accomplishments may steer them further from their objective and overall success.

Shifting objectives can cause mission failure because units equipped and deployed with the right mixture of capabilities for the original objective may not be equipped for any secondary objectives that emerge.

Since military organizations are almost always interdependent, the failure of one unit to accomplish its objective can cause other units to fail as well. Plans may be modified because of enemy actions or other factors, but the objective should remain constant and unchanged except in extenuating circumstances.

Another example of staying on point with the objective came in Operation Desert Storm when the U.S. and its Allies retook Kuwait from Iraq in February 1991. The objective was to drive Saddam Hussein and his military from Kuwait, which they had invaded and occupied a few months prior. In what has been dubbed the "100-Hour War," Coalition Forces were successful in driving out Iraqi forces and retaking Kuwait. However, because they succeeded so quickly, and because Iraq's forces were so decimated, pressure mounted to change the objective from freeing Kuwait to conquering Iraq and disposing of dictator Saddam Hussein.

Whether they should have done this may forever be debated, but let's consider the possible consequences. The Coalition Forces' objective had been attained. To then implement a new objective, though tempting, would have required serious forward planning. The logistics alone of keeping the forces supplied with ammunition, food, water, and other items along the march to Baghdad would have been daunting.

Another consideration had to be our Arab allies in this campaign. They had only signed up to free Kuwait, so to have changed the objective could have split the Coalition's remarkable unity. For the Americans to have changed the objective midstream to include taking all of Iraq could have been interpreted as our real objective all along, potentially damaging America's relations in that region and in the world for a long time.

It can also be much easier to abandon an objective than to keep it, as the subsequent Gulf War would highlight. Not being prepared to occupy territory taken can also be devastating to a force, or at least put it in great danger. The second Gulf War, Operation Iraqi Freedom, had as its objective the occupation of Iraq. Yet this presented a far bigger challenge than simply conquering it.

For these and many other reasons, changing an objective should only be done with careful consideration and planning. And planning needs to go way beyond just creating a new objective.

National Objective

Beginning early in the twentieth century, Marxism had as its objective taking over the world and imposing its agenda on the entire planet. The West had as its objective containment of that expansion which became blurred when the Nixon Administration formulated its relaxed Détente doctrine. This seemed like a reasonable approach but this only worked to the advantage of the Soviets, who had no qualms about violating terms of agreement with the West when it was to their advantage to do so. All they had to do was apologize and keep the West focused on diplomacy rather than its lack of results.

However, President Reagan was a man with core values who saw through these charades. He commissioned a group of policy and intelligence officers to do a competitive analysis study to determine if Détente was the right strategy for dealing with the Soviets. If not, he wanted them to propose alternative strategies. They concluded that Détente was providing a one-sided advantage for the Soviets and that challenging them directly was essential for the objective of containment. They also learned that the Soviet system was so fragile the pressure from such a confrontational strategy could expose these weaknesses, not only eroding its world ambitions but potentially causing its collapse. Reagan saw the wisdom of this approach and implemented a strategy of confrontation rather than appeasement. It worked brilliantly. The Soviet Union collapsed faster than nearly anyone had anticipated.

Reagan's "we win, they lose" objective was not politically correct or popular to those committed to Détente's appeasement strategy. This terrified many on both sides as the beginning of a confrontation that would lead to a nuclear holocaust. Reagan knew the Soviets had never changed their objective to destroy the freedoms and free market systems of the West, so why not resolve to destroy their system?

President Reagan also accomplished something far more important with his new objective—he made our objective clear. The 'Détente' objective of "containment" was ambiguous and clearly not working as communism continued to expand. The clarity of the "we win, they lose" objective may have upset politicians and intellectuals but true leaders were energized by it and the tables turned quickly. Before long the entire Soviet system collapsed.

Wisdom of the Past for the Future

President Reagan came from the World War II generation that had witnessed what Winston Churchill called "an unnecessary war." Obviously, if British and French leaders had had the courage and clarity to confront Hitler even as late as 1938, Nazism could have been defeated at the relatively little cost of 10,000 to 20,000 casualties. However, because of delays caused by the Allies' attempts at appeasement, a confrontation became inevitable two years later at a multiplied casualty cost of some 100 million.

Reagan knew this. He believed, as Churchill did, that such resolve by the West could unravel the Soviet Union without an armed conflict. Reagan formulated this doctrine in his "Evil Empire" speech and held to his objective in the face of abundant opposition and criticism. His objective was accomplished much faster than even he could have imagined when the Iron Curtain collapsed in 1989. His resolve caused the political landscape of the world to change as much as it had after World War II without a physical war.

A Successful Distraction

The principle of a clear and unchanging objective is almost always the proper strategy. Yet too much rigidity in holding to the objective can also lead to failure. The "principles of war" are principles, not laws. Laws cannot be changed; principles have exceptions. That is why leadership is so crucial. Good leaders know how to adapt properly to changing circumstances, which is another principle of war we will cover later—flexibility.

A good example of how holding too lightly to an objective can lead to ultimate failure is the Ford Motor Company. Henry Ford created his company with the objective of building an affordable car to put ownership within the reach of the common people. He met this objective with the "Model T." It became one of the greatest success stories in history. Yet his success nearly became his greatest calamity.

Once we have accomplished our objective, we need another objective to keep advancing. Ford lost sight of the car as the main objective and became obsessed with the process of building it. His advances in assembly line development resulted in advances for all industries. An amazing accomplishment and a primary factor in developing the modern world. Yet it nearly doomed the Ford Motor Company. While Ford became increasingly efficient at building the car, the Model T had become obsolete. This happened because he failed to keep his primary objective with a vision to constantly improve it. This opened the door for a seemingly insignificant car manufacturer, General Motors, to seize the initiative.

The leadership of General Motors could easily copy Ford's improvements on the assembly line, while focusing on making improvements to their product—the car. Ford's sales pitch was you could have any color Model T you wanted so long as it was black. So, General Motors simply introduced new colors and new innovations and improvements to their car with new models coming out every year. Soon the quality and affordability of GM's products eclipsed Ford's, and GM dominated the industry for nearly a century before the Ford Motor Company could catch up.

Again, Ford's innovations with the assembly line benefited the modern world, making him one of the most important innovators of all time. However, his company nearly went bankrupt before he readjusted the focus of his objective—to make great, affordable cars.

Many companies succumb to the pressure of increasing short-term profits at the expense of long-term objectives. Balancing long-term objectives with the short-term pressure of markets is necessary for healthy, continued success. It takes extraordinary leadership to keep both in balance. Still, "The main thing is to keep the main thing the main thing."

Flexible Objectives

For twenty years, the world marveled at why the military of the former Soviet Superpower could not subdue sparse, primitive, and poorly equipped Afghan rebels. There were several reasons, not the least of which was the Soviets ran their war more like a bureaucracy than a military campaign.

For example, Soviet fighters and bombers were given specific targets to hit but were allowed no freedom to deviate from their assigned targets. Because of their cumbersome bureaucratic intelligence, planes would often arrive at their target while enemy forces had since moved on. So, Soviet pilots would obediently drop their bombs on empty ground even with enemy positions in sight.

Later, Soviet pilots explained how frustrating it was to pass up on so many targets because they had to waste their bombs blowing up holes in the ground. Soviet field commanders believed they could have won that campaign quickly and easily had they had freedom to make tactical judgment calls.

Military historians likewise attribute Germany's defeat in World War II to excessive control of tactical operations by Germany's Army High Command or Hitler himself, both of which did not allow the front-line troops to adapt and adjust to fast-changing circumstances on the front. So, how do we balance the need to stay on point with our objective and the need to make feasible, expedient, and tactical level changes?

President Truman once said, "Most people are defeated by secondary successes." By failing to keep focus on the ultimate objective, many get diverted and defeated by lesser secondary opportunities. Had the Soviets not been so overcommitted to hitting primary targets in Afghanistan and allowed their field commanders more flexibility on the ground, their overall objective could have been accomplished, changing the outcome of the war.

Good managers usually want a formula or principle to determine when changes or modifications to the objective are needed. Good leaders know that such a formula or principle cannot be applied to every situation. This is one of those times when leadership must assert itself over principles. Any good computer can tell you the odds of a single formula working for every situation.

There's a Ditch on Either Side of the Right Path

The World War II Battle of Stalingrad is another example of the objective being diverted too quickly to a secondary objective and then holding too tightly to the secondary objective. This was a battle that never should have happened. The German armies could easily have gone around Stalingrad and left a blocking force to contain the Soviet troops there, but Hitler wanted to capture the city because it was named after Stalin.

In this case, the secondary objective was based solely on ego rather than the primary objective of defeating the Soviet Army. Though the latter would have been even more pleasing to the ego. Tenacity and stubbornness may look similar, but they are not. While German forces were stalled fighting for a city with little strategic importance, Hitler became so determined to accomplish his secondary objective it resulted in Germany losing its much larger objective—the war.

If we are copper miners and we strike gold, is it reasonable that we become goldminers? There are times when changing our overall objective makes sense. Holding on to the objective without distraction is important but we also need to hold on to it with flexibility.

We must be disciplined enough to keep our forces and resources focused on the objective without being stupid. This focus is balanced by allowing those on a tactical level to take advantage of opportunities and changing conditions. It is a difficult balancing act. That is why leadership is required, not just rigidly following principles.

That men do not learn very much from the lessons of history is the most important of all the lessons that history has to teach.

– Aldous Huxley

Those who learn from history are the ones most likely to set the course for the future.

– Rick Joyner

Chapter 3

Unity of Command

JB: Once we have established our objective it is easier to design a command structure that is appropriate to the task. We will begin with the military model, understanding that its general principles can be applied and adjusted to our needs.

The military has three basic levels of command:

- Strategic

- Operational

- Tactical

Strategic Level

The strategic level is concerned with the general, overall objective. In World War II, this would have been the Joint Chiefs of Staff whose objective was to defeat the Axis Powers. The Joint Chiefs of Staff in the U.S. do not have direct operational control over forces, but they advise the President, who is the Commander in Chief and the overall leader who must maintain a broad perspective, which in World War II was virtually the entire world.

Emanating from this level of warfare is strategy. Generally speaking, "strategy" is the overarching plan for winning the war campaign. This includes a concept for how to integrate the "elements of National Power" as defined by the Department of Defense toward the goal of victory. These include:

Diplomacy: This focuses on the international goals of the conflict like forming alliances and placating others.

Information: This includes basic factors such as geography, history of the region and/or combatants, and other general relevant information that could affect the conflict, such as local climate and weather patterns.

Intelligence: This includes facts about the opponent's forces, such as resources, lines of communication, potential allies, strategies, and command doctrine.

Military: This includes our assets available for the conflict and those of our adversary.

Economic: This includes broad and/or long-term economic factors that could affect the results of the conflict on either side by limiting supplies which limits endurance.

Law Enforcement: This includes keeping order in occupied territories so violence does not become a distraction, require additional military assets, or attention which could otherwise be devoted to frontline efforts.

A strategic concept includes geopolitical components and military plans. The strategic level requires the military leader to understand national security objectives and to determine how to use military capabilities to accomplish those objectives. Governments develop national security strategy that outline how they will defend themselves and respond to different types of aggression from different sources.

Theater commanders maintain the strategic plans for conflict in their regions. These commanders must also be "big picture" thinkers with broad strategic views of their areas of responsibility. They plan at the macro level and focus on conducting activities that contribute to success at the strategic level. The commander of the U.S. Central Command must be concerned with the big picture of the entire conflict or war, while regional commanders are concerned with specific regions.

Regional commanders must also keep a strategic overview of their region, not just focus on one part of it. For example, the commander for the Middle East theater cannot just maintain focus on ongoing campaigns like Iraq and Afghanistan but must also constantly assess situations in Pakistan, Iran, Syria, Sudan, Yemen, and all other countries in that region.

Neither can the strategic commander allow his attention to be occupied by the ongoing campaigns at the operational level below him. They should obtain reports on these but use them for planning the overall objective for their region, not for giving direct oversight.

Operational Level

Operational level commanders have a narrower focus, concentrating on a particular campaign or grouping of campaigns on a more localized level.

Operational level commanders direct and control the activities of multiple tactical level elements. At this level, campaign objectives are developed, and specific targets identified. Then units are chosen and prepared to take those objectives.

Campaigns often involve multiple types of units, such as infantry, armor, air power, and naval power. They can also involve multinational coalitions. The operational level of warfare requires that commanders apportion forces based on priorities, expected enemy strength to be confronted, and other factors.

Operational level commanders must constantly monitor the progress of campaigns to modify plans, reapportion forces, or shift assets as needed. Should one campaign move more rapidly than expected, the commander must be able to adjust by transferring assets or resources to another campaign that may be progressing more slowly or experiencing greater than expected resistance. They can also react to this scenario by moving forces from the slower-moving group to the one with the greatest potential for breakthrough and thereby achieve a quicker, more decisive victory.

At the operational level, many factors are considered when determining the timing for specific activities to achieve surprise or take advantage of enemy weaknesses. Campaigns may be affected by weather or even when vegetation in the region is most conducive to ground operations. Again, the operational level commander must remain focused on the right factors, not on those at the discretion of the next level up or down.

Tactical Level

The tactical level is the frontline battle where most fighting occurs. Here, the infantry, armor, and other assets encounter the enemy. Here, the mission is to "close with and destroy the enemy by fire, maneuver, or close combat."

The objectives at the tactical level are defined for each fighter whose role in the fight should be easily understood. Teamwork is key to success as is individual valor and initiative. Operational plans are developed and rehearsed when possible.

Tactical commanders must focus on execution of the tactical plan they have been assigned and need not concern themselves with the overall battle or campaign strategy. Their expectation should be that their success will contribute to the overall success of the campaign or war, but they must focus on their part in that plan and know their part in detail.

Tactical level commanders should use their skills and weapons to apply the principles of war to dynamic, fast-paced situations. Taking and holding the initiative requires the enemy to react to you and thereby dictates the battle. However, there are times when we must react to the enemy. The main goal at this level is to systematically reduce the enemy's capabilities and destroy his will to fight. At the tactical level, the warriors must stay focused on destroying the enemy they encounter while eliminating his ability to continue to fight.

Tactical units are often focused on seizing and holding critical terrain for future operations or to deny the enemy its use. Tactical engagements can become intense and personal as each side strives for the annihilation of the other. Commanders must ensure their units are ready, well-supplied, and well-supported for the tactical fight.

Staying in Our Lane

RJ: It is crucial for operations that each commander stay in their lane and not try to do the job of those above or below their level. When commanders fail to do this, the outcome of the engagement can become confused and jeopardized. If a strategic or operational level commander tries to control the tactical fight, such micromanaging can create problems like being distracted from their own task or causing confusion on lower levels.

For commanders to stay within their sphere of authority does not mean they cannot visit the troops for inspections, boost morale, or try to get a better perspective on the situation. Even though an officer may have the authority to give orders directly to anyone under his command, to do so without going through the appropriate lower-level commanders can erode the authority of the lower-level commanders and degrade force effectiveness. Thus, "staying in our lane" is crucial for leadership up and down the chain of command.

Other Applications

These principles can be applied to any enterprise, church, or mission. Industries may have national and international strategies but to be successful they need continuity right down to the local outlet for their products. Success often depends on first identifying and separating the levels of management, then building the right lines of communication between them for smooth application of both strategies and operations.

Just as militaries have a central command that is concerned with operations worldwide and have regional and theater commanders to focus on specific regions or battles, international companies, ministries, and missions usually have a similar chain of authority in their levels of oversight.

Because of various cultures and national government structures, the strategy for marketing in different countries and regions may vary. The melding of these differences into a common strategy can be challenging but manageable with clear spheres of authority when everyone stays in their lane.

The Big Challenge

Resource allotment is usually a major challenge for every organization. In World War II, much was said about the way Patton, the Commander of the U.S. Third Army, and Field Marshal Montgomery, who led the British forces were constantly badgering the overall commander, Eisenhower, for more fuel and supplies for their forces. Both Patton and Montgomery were convinced their battles were the most important for overall victory. From Eisenhower's perspective, both were crucial, and he had to keep both advancing on a uniform front, so the enemy could not exploit large openings between their forces.

It is common for strategic-level commanders or managers to be faced with constant pressure as Eisenhower was. This can also be a sign that things are going the way they should.

Operational and field commanders or managers should be so invested they think their part is the most important and want more resources for their initiative. To help them cope with the rejection of those requests, it is important to give them more insight into the big picture while conveying to them the importance of their sphere of operations.

I (RJ) now run a multifaceted mission organization. We have schools, bases of operations, over five hundred churches and ministries, host up to a dozen conferences a year, publish books and music, produce television shows and other support operations. I like each department head to think theirs is the most important part. Yet many factors can shift this level of importance. Like a good basketball team will recognize when someone has the "hot hand" and give them the ball. I must maintain that same perspective with the different departments in our organization.

I have monthly meetings with our leadership team where I try to keep them informed of the big picture. When one part of the mission becomes important at a particular time, it helps everyone to see why we are focusing effort and resources on that department. However, I do not want my department heads to be overly concerned about things that are not in their lane, while a little knowledge of the big picture helps everyone.

I once had a department head request new electronic equipment. No doubt, it would have made their job easier and helped them produce a better product. Still, with limited resources we must think about all departments. So, I asked that department head to help me find another department that could give up what was needed for this new equipment.

When we went to the first department, our K-12 school, it was determined that to buy this equipment we would have to lay off two teachers. The manager immediately rescinded his request, said he could make do without it, and became more reasonable with all future requests.

I am constantly trying to educate our managers and staff on the factors I must weigh when making decisions. This has also helped them get creative in raising their own resources for things they need. On the other hand, I do not want them carrying the burden for things they can do nothing about. I just need them to focus on their departments and see the big picture enough to know they are only one part of the whole.

However, those at lower levels of command or management often have information and insight which can impact overall strategy. So, the lines of communication need to be as open as possible in both directions. We need to stay in our lanes but not be so rigid that it hurts the free flow of information and initiative.

Crises Bend the Rules

Staying in our lane is important but there are occasions when this can lead to catastrophe. A great example of this was the Battle of Gettysburg in the American Civil War.

General G.K. Warren was credited by President Lincoln for not only saving the Union Army at the Battle of Gettysburg but also for possibly saving the Union. That may seem a stretch but when you understand what he did in this battle and the possible consequences had he not done it, though far outside his lane, he really could have saved the Union.

General Warren was commander of the Corp of Engineers assigned mostly to build bridges and dig trenches. In this battle, he stepped far outside his lane to give orders to combat brigades not under his command. Having completed his own job for the moment, General Warren went on a scouting mission to get a perspective on how the battle might unfold, so his Corp could prepare to build other bridges and defensive positions as needed.

While scouting, General Warren saw that the most strategic point on the battlefield was a hill known as "Little Round Top." He also saw Confederate troops marching into position to seize it. If the Confederates captured Little Round Top their artillery could sweep the Union lines and turn the battle. This could give the Confederate Army a wide avenue to march to Washington and end the war.

Seeing this, General Warren sent messengers with orders to every unit they encountered to get to Little Round Top immediately. They got there just in time with just enough men to hold the position and turn back the Confederate assault. This turned the battle and is still considered one of the most important military operations in U.S. history.

Under normal circumstances, such actions would be unacceptable. General Warren did not have authority to order troops not under his command, but desperate times call for desperate measures. If you do this and save the army and the nation, you will likely be forgiven! Discipline and protocol are critical in the military, but when the situation is grave and obvious, initiative trumps protocol.

General Warren may not have done anything that significant before or after the Battle of Gettysburg, yet

Lincoln noted this one decision may have meant more to the outcome of the war than all other decisions made by all other generals combined.

Summary

Having well-defined boundaries of authority and responsibility are crucial for effective operations within any organization. The larger or more diverse the organization the more critical this becomes. Growth and diversification can allow these boundaries to become murky. This can lead to increasing confusion and conflict within thereby eroding efficiency and effectiveness.

The military accomplishes this by assigning ranks to everyone within the organization. That may not work for a business or church but there are ways to establish as much of this as is necessary for any organization, which we will address later in this study.

The military also has ways for building effectiveness, such as teaching leadership on every level from the lowest private to the highest general. This can be duplicated in many organizations with extraordinary results. With such training, everyone from the lowest to the highest can take personal ownership of their sphere of influence. Plus, training means attention which is interpreted by most as importance, and this builds morale which impacts productivity.

Since everything in an organization reflects the quality and effectiveness of leadership, we will include more examples of this throughout.

I have not failed. I've just found a thousand ways that won't work.

~Thomas Edison

Work begins when the fear of doing nothing at all finally trumps the terror of doing it badly.

~Alain de Botton

Chapter 4

Security

JB: As a principle of war, security is a combination of measures taken to deny the enemy any tactical, operational, or strategic advantage against your forces. In some translations of Clausewitz's book, this is called defense. Security is both active and passive, meaning measures to ensure or enhance security are a combination of both offensive and defensive actions.

It is essential that commanders at all levels implement a comprehensive security plan to deny the enemy information and to detect an enemy's attempt to gain an advantage. A unit in a combat zone must always post sentries when in a static position. That unit might also employ the latest technology to detect any attempt by the enemy to penetrate its perimeter. These are passive measures.

The unit might also conduct patrols around its perimeter to detect enemy encroachments or to engage enemy elements that might be conducting a reconnaissance of the perimeter in preparation for an attack. Furthermore, the unit might actively conduct an array of intelligence collecting activities to identify enemy positions or efforts to gain an advantage. These are all active security measures. A security plan is a critical element of the overall operational plan.

OPERATIONS SECURITY (OPSEC)

Operations security refers to all measures used to deny an enemy information about a unit's intentions, size, disposition, locations, personalities, weapons, equipment, weaknesses, or other elements of knowledge that would aid the enemy.

OPSEC practices include avoiding classified conversations on unclassified systems and communicating with people of unknown reliability about important matters. It also dictates careful handling of classified documents to avoid them falling into enemy hands.

OPSEC procedures require that classified information be passed only to those who need-to-know regardless of their trustworthiness. Once security has been breached, it is impossible to undo the damage, and the more people with classified information is more opportunities for a breach.

Knowing your Adversary

A knowledge of the enemy is essential to providing good security. Enemy tactics and doctrine must be understood. One must study the enemy and know him. A known and predictable enemy is much easier to defeat than one that is unknown, or prone to do the unexpected. An enemy that follows his own doctrine is more vulnerable than one that does not, assuming you are familiar with that doctrine. Know your foe.

Time must be spent studying and contemplating the enemy to understand how he fights and to assess his vulnerabilities. This knowledge of the enemy provides security to the friendly commander and his forces. Any attempt to anticipate the next move by the enemy should be supported by a careful analysis of previous enemy actions or reactions. Knowing how the enemy has acted in the past is a good indicator of what to expect in the future; however, we cannot totally depend on this.

The Security Screen

RJ: Navy frigates were designed for multiple purposes because they were smaller vessels with good maneuverability. One of their primary missions was to patrol the perimeter of their fleet to protect it from a surprise attack. Naval commanders did not want to be surprised by an enemy fleet on the horizon. They wanted and needed early warnings of approaching enemy ships. The frigates were tasked with sailing on the flanks and to the front and rear of the fleet to provide these early warnings.

Of course, as technology developed, Navy frigates were given powerful radar that could reach far beyond the horizon to detect threats. Fleets now have AWACS (Airborne Warning and Control Systems) far beyond the frigates' detection abilities, which can reach hundreds of miles further providing even more security for the fleet and for ground forces. These are now also supplemented with satellites which have remarkable capabilities for providing security for our forces and homeland.

Likewise, in the past, cavalries played a similar role in protecting ground forces. Mounted on horses, the cavalry was highly mobile and adept at detecting approaching enemy infantry and cavalry. Since the earliest recorded accounts of warfare, security has been a fundamental principle of war that commanders have stressed in their plans and ensured through their actions. Good security is a key factor in ensuring victory. Regardless of how brilliant our offensive actions may be, we can still be doomed if we fail to provide adequate security for our forces.

Initiative

The security of your base and forces is crucial, but once these are adequate, the emphasis needs to be on launch offensive operations. Defense can help put you in a place for offensive operations, but you cannot win on defense. You must change the defensive mentality to an offensive one to win. This is called "taking the initiative." To take and keep the initiative is essential for victory. Once you have the initiative, your opponent must constantly react, so now you dictate the action.

For this reason, security is a fundamental principle of war. It is also one we want to make secondary in our thinking and planning as quickly and as feasible as possible once it is adequately accomplished.

Applying Security to Business, Missions, etc.

In our increasingly technological world, there is a need to constantly upgrade technical security. This includes securing your files from hackers seeking to steal your plans, research, and other factors that could compromise your advantage in the market. Large organizations that can afford to often hire former military or intelligence officers to build a military or intelligence type of security for their company. This has become increasingly necessary in the increasingly interconnected world we live in.

Smaller organizations can have near top-level security because security itself has become a major industry sector in which many companies now serve. They can be contracted to evaluate weaknesses in your security, propose actions that will strengthen your security, and monitor your operations regularly to help you stay ahead of threats.

Since Christianity is increasingly persecuted around the world, security is an increasing consideration for churches and Christian missions as well. Churches, synagogues, and mosques have become common targets for mass shootings, bombings, and other attacks. Consequently, regular security audits are becoming essential. Church leaders are called "shepherds" and a shepherd's basic duty is the security of the flock.

Good security requires the right people directing it. Good security personnel will forever be studying the attacks that have happened to others and using this information to check their own vulnerabilities. They will also stay current on new security technologies to understand and maintain the level of proficiency and strategy needed for their situation.

Security is addressed before other operational and offensive principles of war because, without it, all other plans and actions may be rendered useless.

Don't be an if thinker, be a how thinker... Don't count your days, make your days count... It is the will to win that counts, and not the wish to win.

– Dale Brown

Chapter 5

Maneuver

JB: The military principle of maneuver is defined as the movement and positioning of forces to gain an advantage over the enemy. Commanders use the maneuver principle to attack an enemy's weaknesses before the enemy can react, or to disrupt an enemy's attempt to exploit its own weaknesses.

Sometimes a maneuver is planned, other times it is spontaneous. A commander may choose to execute a maneuver when he sees an opportunity to defeat or severely damage enemy forces. Sometimes a maneuver is executed to thwart an enemy's attempt to attack one's vulnerabilities. Thus, keeping one's forces flexible and always ready to maneuver is essential.

To take advantage of the principle of maneuver, commanders must continually be aware of their opponent's actions and disposition. This requires current intelligence on the enemy. A robust plan must be developed for how an enemy will be constantly monitored through every source of intelligence collection at the commander's disposal, so he can choose the precise time and location to maneuver his forces.

The commander must also maintain adequate flexibility in his operational plan to maneuver as needed. Commanders usually maintain a reserve element that is positioned precisely for that purpose. The reserve is not initially engaged in the battle but remains in position close to the front so they can maneuver rapidly as needed, especially when a breach in the enemy's line occurs, or to respond to a danger the enemy has created, or another opportunity arises.

The principle of maneuver may also be used to deceive an adversary or exploit a success by friendly forces. Before maneuvering, a commander must make sure his troops know the purpose of their actions. For example, if their purpose is to deceive the enemy to keep them from perceiving the true intentions of friendly forces, the maneuvering unit needs to know this.

A trick maneuver may move intentionally slow to ensure the enemy sees it and responds in a way that opens a weakness in their defenses. Or, if a maneuver by a friendly force is designed to attack an exposed flank of the enemy it may need to be executed rapidly before the enemy can react. So, the speed and pace of the maneuver is important.

At times, a maneuver may be designed to simply fix the enemy in one place, while the main attack of friendly forces occurs elsewhere. Such an action can prevent the enemy from executing a maneuver of his own since he must keep his troops in place to defend his position from threatening forces.

A commander must go into each engagement expecting his enemy to do something that will give him an opportunity to maneuver his forces and strike a lethal blow or dislodge the enemy from his position. Maneuver is such a critical factor that most battles are won by the side that is most adept at maneuvering.

Likewise, a slow or poorly executed maneuver can cause an attack to fail or give the enemy time to react with an effective counter maneuver. Leaders must be decisive and aggressive when executing a maneuver, especially when the maneuver is intended to eliminate the opponent.

Maneuver Saved the Union

RJ: On July 2, 1863, Colonel Joshua Lawrence Chamberlain and his 20th Maine Regiment executed one of the most famous maneuvers in U.S. military history. As the Battle of Gettysburg continued into its second day, the Union forces occupied Cemetery Ridge just outside the small town of Gettysburg. Confederate forces advanced on the left flank of the Union Army. All they had to do was dislodge the Union soldiers from the high ground to take the small hill known as Little Round Top. This would allow Confederate forces to roll up the Union flank and wreak havoc where their logistics and artillery were located. This also could have allowed Confederate forces to march into Washington unchecked and end the war.

Colonel Chamberlain and the 20th Maine were on the extreme left end of the maneuvering brigade, holding the left flank of Union forces. Colonel Chamberlin and his men trotted quickly to their positions and began an immediate defense of Little Round Top. After two devastating charges by Confederate forces, Colonel Chamberlain's regiment of three hundred eighty-five men had been reduced to half strength and were running out of ammunition. Knowing he could not withstand another frontal assault by Confederate forces, Chamberlain ordered the famous "pinwheel maneuver" where his men swung around like a gate, followed by a bayonet charge into the ranks of the Confederates. In what looked like a suicide charge by his superiors looking down from the top of the hill, the maneuver amazingly broke the Confederate advance and saved Little Round Top from capture.

Maneuver Saves the Allies

Similarly, during the Nazi counterattack on the Western Front during World War II that became known as the "Battle of the Bulge," the Germans had surrounded the American 101st Airborne Division at the strategic crossroads town of Bastogne. The German advance could not bypass the town and leave such a force in its rear, so they were stalled until they could either destroy the 101st or get them to surrender. In one of the most heroic stands of the war, the 101st held against the vastly superior force that surrounded them. Though they suffered constant assaults and bombardment they could not be broken. As the 101st ran low on ammunition and supplies, neither side thought they could last much longer, that is, until one of the most brilliant maneuvers of the entire war saved them.

Meanwhile, in a war council, General Patton said he could disengage his army from another battle, turn it, and march to relieve Bastogne within three days. When a British general asked Patton how he could pull off such an extraordinary maneuver, Patton replied, he had trained his men well and they could do it. Eisenhower agreed to let him try, and to everyone's astonishment, Patton was in Bastogne three days later, relieving the 101st Airborne and breaking the entire German attack.

A remarkable footnote to this battle was when Patton's forces broke through the German lines to link up with the 101st, the men of the 101st said they were relieved to see their fellow soldiers but "did not need rescuing." They thought they were "doing just fine" holding the German army at bay and were not even close to surrendering.

The 101st was called "the point of the spear" of the Allied forces, which became the basis for the classic television series *Band of Brothers*. Those who knew them said they were one of the toughest and most resourceful divisions the Allies had. Nevertheless, this astonishing maneuver by Patton's forces to disengage on one front, turn ninety degrees, and make it to Bastogne in only three days, broke the courage and resolve of the Germans to continue their assault. The German forces surrendered in large numbers, and a few months later, the war with Germany was over.

Foundations for Maneuver

The two foundations of the strategy of maneuver are readiness and courage. Colonel Chamberlain's amazing Pinwheel Maneuver against a superior force with little or no ammunition was pure heroism. He had been told his regiment was the flank of the entire Union Army which must be held at all costs. He resolved to do exactly that.

Colonel Chamberlain was not a professional soldier. He had been an English professor before the war, and was elected Colonel of his regiment, not because of any military training or competence, but because of his popularity among Maine's troops. He took this honor seriously and devoted himself to living up to the trust of his men by becoming the best leader he could be. He studied combat and battle strategies continually and constantly trained his men to carry them out. When the time came, his courage proved to match his devotion to study.

The saying is true, "There are many soldiers, but not many warriors." Colonel Chamberlain proved to be one of the greatest warriors in American military history. After being promoted to Brigadier General, he went on to distinguish himself by his intelligence, coolness under fire and maneuvers, and resolve to accomplish every objective assigned to him. He often did this with brilliant innovations and maneuvers which caught his opponents off guard and left them vulnerable.

Some who have been raised in military schools and academies may be effective at training and preparing troops for combat, but do not do well under the tension and intensity of combat. They may be soldiers, but they are not warriors. Others are born for warfare. They excel when pressure is greatest as Chamberlain did. They are warriors.

Good soldiers are needed in the military even if they are not born warriors. They may still accomplish great things, display great courage, and be the backbone of our forces. However, in the heat of battle, the warriors become evident. In battle, soldiers who outrank them will often turn to the warriors for counsel and even leadership. In battle, many have taken authority beyond their pay grade to seize the initiative or meet a crisis. This is usually done by executing a bold and unexpected maneuver that is invisible to the timid.

General Patton was known to have a big ego and admitted to being a prima donna, but he was a warrior whom some consider the best field commander the Allies had. In the above noted war council, when the Allied command was considering what could be done to relieve Bastogne and stop the German counter offensive, the men who sat in that room knew they were in danger of defeat. So, when Patton said he could relieve Bastogne and break the German attack, one of the officers said what most were thinking—it was impossible. It was also well known that Patton's men did not like him. Patton replied, he was not concerned whether his men liked him—he only wanted them to fight for him, and he had trained them to do just that. That's a warrior mentality. They are not in a popularity contest—they are focused on what it takes to win.

This does not mean warriors cannot be liked by their men. Chamberlain was loved by his men, as was General Robert E. Lee, Napoleon, and many other great warriors in history. However, warriors are not controlled by what their men think of them and often disregard public opinion.

Likewise, leaders are not overly concerned with safety. If they were, bold strategies, tactics, and maneuvers required to win battles would not be available to them. The key word here is "overly." Chamberlain's bold maneuver cost the lives of many he dearly loved, including his own brother. The most successful boldest maneuvers are also the costliest. To counter this, we must also consider the cost of defeat if we did not act with boldness.

In war, the consequence of failure is counted in lives and perhaps nations and cultures. Likewise, it takes courage to lead a business when decisions can cost jobs and livelihoods. So, like a general in battle, risks must be weighed against possible reward when considering a maneuver.

"Custer's Last Stand"

George Armstrong Custer is best known for "Custer's Last Stand" at the Battle of Little Big Horn. However, a study of Custer's military career makes it clear that "standing" was not Custer's best characteristic. He was constantly moving, maneuvering, and his exploits in the Civil War are some of the greatest examples of just how powerful maneuver can be.

At the Battle of Gettysburg, Custer was the youngest general in the Union Army but his contribution to the Union's victory may have been equally important as General Warren's or Colonel Chamberlain's. As is often true in battle, there can be many maneuvers that combine to achieve victory, and many heroes that save the force from defeat and make victory possible.

After two days of fighting, the Battle of Gettysburg had already been one of the costliest of the war for both sides. Still, neither army had gained an advantage over the other. General Lee was determined to break that stalemate with one of his boldest maneuvers yet. He sent his cavalry, led by Jeb Stuart, around to attack Union forces from the same point behind where Pickett would advance from the front. Had Stuart completed this maneuver, Union forces would almost certainly have been cut in two and suffered a defeat that could have ended the war.

While on patrol, Custer saw Stuart's forces approaching the rear of the Union center, and with a greatly inferior force charged with such ferocity that Stuart's cavalry was turned back. Without Stuart's attack from the rear, Pickett's men marched into a devastating trap in what became known as the "high-water mark of the Confederacy." Instead of winning the battle and likely the war, this one failed maneuver was the beginning of the end for the South.

It was also Custer's brilliant maneuvering at the end of the siege of Petersburg that led to Lee's army being dislodged from its seemingly impregnable defenses. A few days later, it was Custer's continued brilliant maneuvering that cut off Lee's retreat and forced the Battle of Sailor's Creek, the last major battle of the war. This battle devastated Lee's remaining forces. Then again, it was Custer's brilliant maneuvering that cut off the retreat of Lee's remaining forces, forcing him to surrender. Without a doubt Custer's brilliance in using the mobility of his cavalry to maneuver was a primary factor in the Union's victory.

Out Maneuvered

Custer's aggressiveness served him well in the Civil War and the subsequent Indian wars until the Battle of Little Big Horn. Many times, his bold maneuvering tactics allowed him to get away with charging ahead without thoroughly evaluating the terrain. This is a basic violation of military procedure and wisdom, but Custer's victories made it difficult to argue with his tactics. Yet one time he was not in the right place at the right time with the right force against a vastly superior force and paid the ultimate price for violating these basic rules.

Too much or too easy success can lead to pride which always comes before a fall. Pride blinds while humility keeps us vigilant. Custer's Last Stand was such a humiliating defeat, and he is known more for this one defeat than for all his great victories combined, some of which are still considered among the greatest in U.S. military history. This one defeat is also studied more than all his victories. It may not be fair, yet that is often the result of being careless and arrogant. The rewards for being bold and successful can be great, and you will be celebrated if you succeed. Similarly, the cost of being bold but unsuccessful can be even higher.

We will cover this more in depth later, but defense never wins a war. It can help keep you fighting until conditions change and you can go on offense, but to win you must go on the offense at some point, and that requires maneuvering.

Other Applications for Maneuver

In business, we frequently hear about companies that are not doing well, and then suddenly a bold, new initiative or product turns their fortunes around. Many of the popular products we now have like automobiles and electronic devices were born out of this pressure that makes maneuver a critical strategy. Hardship or impending doom can wonderfully focus our attention to where some of our greatest creativity is found. This gives birth to maneuvers which can change our trajectory.

To take advantage of disadvantage, we must have the mindset we will prevail. When danger is joined by courage, resolve, and faith, it releases creativity. It is the lack of faith that saps our creativity, so we must not allow this type of thinking. Thinking of how we can maneuver often leads to other possibilities which can lead to a change of outcome.

The story is often related how an American general responded when reports came in that his forces had been surrounded. He reportedly said, "Great. Attack in every direction. They won't get away this time!"

During his career, General Douglas MacArthur experienced some devastating defeats, yet his brilliant and innovative maneuvers produced some of the greatest victories in both World War II and in the Korean War.

Likewise, it was MacArthur's seeming arrogance toward his abilities, and his scorn for the intelligence that China was about to enter the war in Korea, that became the great general's own undoing. The U.N. forces were soundly defeating the North Koreans and driving them back when hundreds of thousands of Chinese poured across the border and into the fight. Then the U.N. forces were close to being defeated, if not destroyed.

This same type of arrogance displayed by MacArthur resulted in Custer's force being destroyed. Some of the most devastating defeats in history have followed great victories, which often led to carelessness and arrogance. Yet MacArthur did not give up and used more brilliant maneuvering to rescue his forces until they could go back on the offensive. Unfortunately, he was relieved of duty, leaving these maneuvers to his successor.

Creativity and Maneuver

If you are in a crowd, unless you're the tallest, you cannot see further than those in front of you. Likewise, those who stand tallest in history are those who can see past what others see and have the courage to take bold action. Maneuver is the special domain of those who have vision and the boldness to take initiative.

Years ago, it was reported that some corporations were considering not hiring college graduates because the present education system conditioned students so they could not think creatively or "outside the box." By the way, this happened when public schools started favoring indoctrination over education, rewarding mediocrity, and penalizing initiative and creativity. To survive much less prosper in today's world, we must break out of the mental shackles modern education places on students to learn and think creatively. To do this, we must be able to see into the future. To succeed requires courage to take bold action, and those who can see into the future the clearest and act with the most creativity, have a great advantage because those are the characteristics most needed to effectively maneuver.

No Where to Go but Up

The greatest maneuvers in history came from those willing to step outside the box and go beyond tradition to act on what they envisioned. Most of them had such desperation that outrageous actions and boldness became their only option.

At Valley Forge, George Washington saw his army melting away as winter dragged on. His army was so poorly equipped few even had shoes. At this lowest point, he considered it a good time to attack the enemy. It was a brilliant maneuver that likely saved the Revolution.

Washington's maneuver was to cross the Delaware River and capture the entire force of Hessian troops in Trenton, New Jersey with a surprise attack. News of this bold strike and resounding victory went throughout the colonies and within weeks Washington's force had swelled to many times its previous size. Then after years of suffering more continuous defeats, it took just one more successful maneuver for Washington to box in the British Army at Yorktown, force their surrender, and win the war.

Since "the Great Recession" that began in 2008, many companies, charities, missions, and churches have been struggling to survive, and some have lost the battle. In 2020, the whole world was virtually crippled by the coronavirus pandemic. Already many companies, churches, and other organizations are disappearing because they could not maneuver fast enough or well enough to counter this crisis. Like all other crises, when this is all over, it will be the ones that were agile and bold enough to maneuver that not only survived but also prospered.

The person who believes that he can do something is probably right, and so is the person who believes that he can't.

– Unknown

Chapter 6

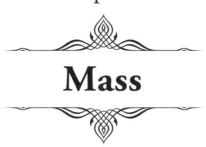

Mass

JB: Mass is the principle of bringing a concentration of forces and combat power against an enemy at a critical time and location to create a breakthrough. If a breakthrough is created in the enemy lines, they must retreat or be surrounded and allow their supplies to be overrun. This also places them in the untenable position of being attacked from multiple directions at once.

The principle of mass has changed over time. During the Napoleonic wars, large armies faced off on the battlefield in close formation. Mass was the primary method used as each side tried to gather an overwhelming force, at some point, to break through their opponent's lines. The winner was frequently determined by who could maneuver the most effectively to apply overwhelming numbers at a specific point on the battlefield. There are many examples of smaller forces winning a battle simply by being more maneuverable. This enabled them to mass in a place or time their foe could not counter and create a breakthrough.

The Goal—Breakthrough

RJ: During the American Civil War, the concept of mass was based on assembling large numbers of dismounted troops, horse mounted cavalry, and artillery at a place on the battlefield. The idea was to wear down the opposing lines by attrition, then break through those lines with an attack. After an artillery barrage at the planned point of attack, the massed troops were deployed in depth so rear troops could pass through the first wave once a breach had been created. Massed formations supported by artillery were a difficult tactic for an unprepared defender to repel.

Today's technology and the lethality of modern weaponry have caused a shift in the methodology for massing against an enemy. Airpower is a force multiplier. Artillery and bombing by close air support provide smaller forces a much greater ability to successfully engage an enemy with superior numbers. Massing the full capabilities of a military force today includes combining airpower, ground forces, artillery, rocket launchers, attack helicopters, armor, as well as unmanned aerial and robotic vehicles. Combined these present a formidable force capable of defeating a numerically superior enemy.

When a battlefield commander masses his forces, it reflects his expectation of achieving victory, or at least accomplishing a critical objective. Commanders must carefully assess the situation before deciding where and when to mass their forces. A commander must consider the enemy's strengths and weaknesses, as well as those of his own forces. A commander's plan should go beyond the defeat of enemy forces to include exploiting a breakthrough and success by pursuing the enemy and continuing to destroy his formations, support, and morale.

General MacArthur used the principle of mass very effectively in September 1950 at Inchon, South Korea. When the North Koreans attacked their neighbors to the south in June 1950, the South Korean Army began a rapid retreat southward toward Pusan. On July 5, the U.S. began to land Army forces at Pusan Harbor to halt the retreat of the South Koreans and begin a counterattack to push the North Koreans back. As "Task Force Smith" (named for the Battalion Commander of the five-hundred-forty-man unit) disembarked and began executing combat operations, it became obvious to General MacArthur that the task would be difficult and that the counterattack from the "Pusan Perimeter" must be supported by a larger offensive from a different part of South Korea. He felt he needed to strike decisively at the North Korean flanks or rear, and that his operation needed to be a clear victory for U.N. forces and a clear threat to the entire North Korean Army to force its retreat. MacArthur knew that only through massing forces at this critical time and location could he achieve such success.

MacArthur chose the port city of Inchon with its notoriously large and unforgiving tides to mass his invasion force and break through the North Korean defenses. It was also where they would least expect an attack. It worked brilliantly. His troops overwhelmed the North Korean resistance and forced the North Korean Army to begin a rapid retreat north to prevent being cut off. MacArthur massed at the right time and the right place, turned the situation completely around and put the invading North Koreans on the defensive.

The Risk of Mass

In the American Civil War, Confederate General Lee used the strategy of mass in "Pickett's Charge" at the Battle of Gettysburg. He was not successful because a major part of his strategy, the attack of Stuart's Calvary from the rear of the Union Army, was thwarted by Custer's attack on Stuart. Though this is a basic strategy used for victory in nearly any combat situation, it does have its risks. At Gettysburg, Lee had a two-pronged attack, which could have doubled his chance for victory were it successful. However, this would also double his risk if half his force was restrained from completing its part. Mass is a simple strategy that is best kept simple and well within a force's capabilities.

If your plan requires several, complicated parts to succeed, then you are likely setting yourself up for defeat. Rarely does everything go as planned in combat. If your plan is well within your capabilities, you will have plenty of reserve for surprises and contingencies. Lee's strategy had little hope of success unless everything went perfectly. It did not.

The first problem Lee encountered was his preliminary bombardment before the attack. It was possibly the most intense cannonade of the war but also the least effective because it was aimed at where he thought the Union reserves were massed instead of where they were. Lee assumed the Union reserves were behind the front lines, but Union General Meade had anticipated this and moved them all to the front line. So, possibly the biggest cannonade of the war fell on empty ground. Pickett's division then charged into a virtually unmolested front. With the needed perfect timing of Stuart's attack thwarted and the cannonade ineffective,

Lee's attack based on mass resulted in a massive slaughter of Confederate forces.

Logistics and the Strategy of Mass

Napoleon was one of the most successful generals in history because of his brilliant use of the strategy of mass. His use was superior to his opponents because he had devised a very fast and efficient method of supplying troops. This enabled his forces to move faster and mass faster than his enemies could counter. At times, he even moved entire divisions from one end of the battlefield to the other—a concept his adversaries would not even consider because they could not move their supplies and troops quickly enough. And troops cannot move without ammunition, food, and water.

Mass Countering Mass

In the final year of World War I, it seemed all conditions favored a German breakthrough and victory. After the collapse of Russia on the Eastern Front, Germany could move all its troops from the Eastern Front and mass for a breakthrough Spring offensive. Both sides expected the German Spring offensive to overwhelm the worn-out British and French forces, and just brush aside the less-experienced Americans. The assault went as expected the first few weeks with the British and French being pushed back miles beyond their previous positions. However, the German attack began to falter as their supply lines became so extended, they could not keep the needed supplies flowing to the front. They began to lose the initiative.

Then the Supreme Commander, French General Foch, released the American Army under General Pershing to mass and assault what had been considered impregnable German forces in the Ardennes Forest. The Americans suffered heavy casualties but continued pressing until the stretched German lines broke. Just a few weeks after the Allies were expected to lose the war, Germany surrendered. Both armies used the strategy of mass, but one used it more effectively and won the war.

Mass Marketing

Once a breakthrough is created, it is crucial to keep the initiative and keep the adversary on the defensive, unable to devise their own plans that would enable them to regain the initiative.

This strategy of mass to create a breakthrough is also crucial for business, missions, and virtually any enterprise. Creating a product breakthrough is usually achieved by advertising. Sporadic advertising is seldom effective. Advertising should be conducted like a military campaign using mass to gain the initiative and breakthrough, then continuing the initiative until complete success is achieved.

Of course, many factors contribute to a successful advertising campaign, such as branding and messaging which can attract potential customer interest. However, most important is to have a superior product. Using the strategy of mass for marketing also requires having the resources to create a breakthrough and keep the momentum going. Now with instant communication through technology and social media, all that is needed to keep the forward momentum is satisfied customers telling others.

Mass Movements

Mass movements are one of the most powerful shapers of culture and the trajectory of civilization. Gladwell's book *The Tipping Point* addressed some of the causes that make things "go viral." One interesting factor is that no amount of advertising can cause this—true mass comes from the masses.

Even Gladwell's book leaves many unanswered questions about this phenomenon. One reason is that every mass movement is unique. To understand them, we must discern common characteristics. Yet the next mass movement is still likely to be unique and come from unexpected sources.

Some mass movements erupt suddenly and unexpectedly. Others build over time, or even generations. The fast-appearing ones are the most spectacular but can disappear as fast as they appeared. The sweeping appearance of hula hoops was spectacular and perhaps unprecedented, but their quick disappearance was no less so. One day they were everywhere. The next day they seemed to disappear.

Slow-growing mass movements take longer to gain momentum but can have so much mass behind them they become difficult to stop. Things that happen fast rarely have depth or longevity. This leaves us with some strategic and tactical decisions to make about mass movements.

The best we can do with mass movements that just happen is try and give them some direction. With many mass movements, the so-called leaders are not leading at all. They're just trying to keep up with the masses. However, one thing history teaches us is that a vacuum of leadership will ultimately be filled—good or bad. So, how can mass movements be directed once they have started and gained momentum? Because they are so unique, most certainly by creativity and boldness.

Mass movements can be ignited by a leader, but they can also run over their leader if the leader stops moving in the direction they are going, as many political movements have. It's like riding a tiger—you may get carried a long way, or you may get eaten along the way.

There are people who feed mass movements and there are people who feed off them. A friend of mine, who was one of the best-selling Christian authors of all time, once told me his job was to discern which way the Holy Spirit was moving and get there before He did and set up a book table! He was only half joking because he was one who both fed and fed off movements. His books and leadership helped steer movements through the 1970s and 1980s, yet he admitted he was being carried along with everyone else.

There are also leaderless mass movements started and led by the masses that do not respond well to anyone steering them. A mass movement that is shallow and weak will often melt quickly under the heat of scorn or criticism, but those with depth will not. All will be criticized, which weeds out the unworthy and unnecessary movements.

Mass movements can be exciting or scary. They can be used for good or bad, and sometimes both. Two mass movements that created the most death, pain, and suffering in history were the Nazi and Marxist/communist movements. Both were born out of bitterness and fed on people's bitterness and discontent.

Hitler did not start the Nazi movement but joined it when it was small and still forming its identity. Seeing a vacuum of leadership, Hitler quickly filled it. He galvanized his base by feeding their discontent and even more by giving them specific enemies to blame for their problems. Foundations are important, and this one was evil from the beginning.

The socialist/communist movement began much like the Nazi movement—igniting and feeding people's bitterness and discontent. They grew as they began to blame and target specific enemies, mostly their upper merchant classes and nobility.

We can go back further and find the roots of both these movements in the French Revolution, which happened just after the American Revolution. Though some goals of these revolutions were similar, the French Revolution descended into a crazed madness and evil that shocked the world. When the French Revolution sought to declare immediate equality and distribution of wealth and authority, this led to chaos which ultimately opened the door for an even more severe dictatorship than the king—Napoleon.

The American Revolution was unique in history in that it was led by the wealthiest people in the colonies but produced the first Constitutional Republic. It also produced more liberty and opportunity than any nation before it. This was not without flaws and contradictions to its declared mandate to treat all people equally, but it also permitted the liberties needed to confront these inconsistencies and bring the needed corrections.

How did the American Revolution succeed while the French Revolution failed? The American Republic was devoted to providing equal opportunity rather than equal outcome. Anyone could be successful in America, but they had to work hard for it. In the French Revolution, the goal shifted to making everyone equal by taking from the successful and distributing their wealth. Such a philosophy may sound noble to the ignorant and idealistic, but it has never created anything except the destruction of every culture or civilization that has tried it. Only the most primitive cultures can survive a basic distribution of everything equally because they are small and simple.

The mass movement that fueled the American Revolution did create a breakthrough, which could have gone bad had some not stayed focused on the reason for the movement—a representation of the will of the people in government. When the American Revolutionary War began, the American Patriots already had an idea of what kind of government they wanted before defeating the British. The French had no such idea. So, when they seized power, chaos and anarchy reigned.

When the American Revolutionary War was won, it was not the end of the fight but in many ways the beginning of a more difficult battle to construct a government and constitution that would last. This struggle continues to this day.

This is also an important lesson about movements. Creating a mass movement is an accomplishment, but it will accomplish little if we do not have a good plan for the sequel. Many of the greatest accomplishments in history came through mass movements, but a key to significant and lasting accomplishment is the ability to keep the movement moving.

An optimist sees an opportunity in every calamity and a pessimist sees a calamity in every opportunity.

– Winston Churchill

Chapter 7

Surprise

JB: Surprise is used to catch an enemy off guard and put him in a vulnerable situation. It can also be used to disrupt an enemy's attack. Surprise is doing the unexpected or doing the expected in an unexpected way.

Surprise requires a commander's creativity and boldness. One who can think creatively has an advantage over an adversary who cannot. If you can constantly surprise your foe or competitor, you are more likely to take and hold the initiative which is necessary for ultimate victory.

RJ: Surprise must be backed by sound planning, or you may suddenly find yourself surprised and at a disadvantage. All principles of war are closely intertwined, and the principle of surprise is closely tied to the principle of security. Surprise attacks or maneuvers have historically been the most effective principles for achieving victory, but they can also lead to serious dangers. It is not a lack of faith in your plan or in those carrying it out to have contingency plans. Remember, the enemy also gets a vote, so never go into an operation without contingencies.

Commanders often go to great lengths to achieve surprise. They can design elaborate deception plans to mask their true plan of attack. No commander wants his adversary to know his intentions. If your tactical or operational plan becomes known to your enemy, it can give him an opportunity to build a defense or even a surprise counterattack. Using multiple surprise strategies and tactics can keep the enemy guessing about your true intentions. As technology continues to advance, the ability to achieve strategic surprise is diminished, while the use of technology to aid in achieving surprise at the operational or tactical level can be a powerful tool.

Achieving surprise usually results in a swift victory with less casualties. The principle of surprise is also the main factor that allows commanders to fight and win against superior forces. So, if your resources are less than your opponent, you should be even more devoted to using the strategy of surprise.

Deception is usually employed to achieve surprise, such as when a boxer maneuvers with one hand to draw his opponent's attention, so he can sneak in a blow with the other hand. Many techniques and tactics have been developed to deceive opponents. Today's militaries have significant capability to conduct military deception using sophisticated equipment and technology. It is even possible to create a "phantom" force unit electronically. With the proper equipment, a military unit can duplicate the electronic signature of a large unit where none exists and create the impression of an impending attack while the real attack comes from a different position or direction.

Of course, an enemy lacking good security is most vulnerable to a surprise attack. Also, when the enemy is predictable, it's easier to develop a reasonable plan to surprise him. For this reason, it is imperative to study your opponent's tactics and doctrine.

A good intelligence program that keeps a close watch on the enemy is critical for knowing which surprise tactics will likely be effective. Knowing what an adversary is doing, or what his intentions are, enhances our odds of surprising him. Intelligence is information about the enemy that has been analyzed and is therefore considered to have a high degree of accuracy and reliability.

As noted, on December 25, 1776, George Washington turned the direction of the Revolutionary War from almost certain defeat to what would become ultimate victory. He did this by masterfully using the tactic of surprise. Washington and his poorly equipped troops had been defeated in New York and pushed all the way to Philadelphia. The British ceased operations for the winter, assuming the Americans had done the same. Leaving Hessian mercenaries to guard Trenton, New Jersey, the senior British commanders and much of their force returned to New York to enjoy a time of rest and festivities before returning in the Spring to resume their campaign against the patriots.

Washington knew he must strike a decisive blow to improve his sagging troop morale and boost the confidence of the colonists to continue the fight. Since the Hessians assumed the Continental Army would use the winter break to recuperate from their recent defeats, they did little to prepare defensive positions. Instead, the Hessians took the opportunity to celebrate Christmas with drinking and partying.

Washington perceived the opportunity. He had an inferior force, so he had to rely almost totally on surprise. Crossing the icy Delaware River under the cover of darkness, General Washington's small army was able to completely surprise the Hessians. The Hessian commander, General Jahl, was forced to surrender the entire garrison, giving the Continental Army the greatly needed victory and supplies. Washington could accomplish this because he knew his enemy could anticipate their actions and was willing to employ a tactic he had not used before.

Before Washington made the attack, he conducted extensive reconnaissance operations to be sure of his strategy and have an accurate analysis of Hessian vulnerabilities. Still, surprise was the most important element of his plan and he used it successfully to his advantage.

Surprise does not have to be total to be effective. The Allied invasion of France on D-Day was not a total surprise. In fact, it was expected. Where the surprise came was the Allies had created a fictitious army and used a brilliant counterintelligence scheme to convince the Germans the main attack would come in northwest France near Calais. Therefore, when the attack came in Normandy, the Germans were convinced it was a diversionary attack to draw their forces away from the real attack, which kept the bulk of their forces in the wrong place. This allowed the Allies to get enough forces ashore to establish a defense that could repel the German counterattack.

In one of General Lee's most brilliant victories in the Civil War Battle of Chancellorsville, he used surprise. He created this surprise by violating another basic military doctrine—never divide your forces. The Union commanders who were engaged with Lee on one front never expected the attack by an entire Corp from a different direction. This surprise threw the entire Union Army into disarray and retreat.

Lee was a genius at using the principle of surprise because he knew he otherwise had no chance against a Union Army with superior numbers and resources. Surprise can be a great equalizer.

Surprise in Marketing

Successful companies have also learned to use the principle of surprise to their advantage. Their research and development of new products are often as closely guarded as military secrets. To be first to market a new product has a huge advantage. Apple has been one of the most recent companies to effectively use this strategy. From the iPhone and iPad to a continuous stream of innovations, they have kept their competitors surprised and at bay for years.

Only a small percentage of people are trendsetters and innovators. They are almost always the first to try new things. If you can attract trendsetters, they often have much influence over the masses, who are followers rather than trendsetters. For this reason, wise companies will only release word about a new product or innovation when they are convinced they are far ahead of any potential competitor. Then when they do, they especially target trendsetters in their marketing, knowing there is no more powerful commercial than talk and excitement.

Surprise as a Lifestyle

Boredom in the workplace can be bad for morale, and that can have a direct impact on creativity and productivity. The most successful startups in recent years have mostly been high tech and new tech. Studies of these reveal an important common denominator—a vibrant and exciting workplace that is conducive to creativity which nearly always creates surprises.

The natural world is infinitely diverse. It is believed that every snowflake is unique, as is every leaf on a tree and every person on the planet. There is no one else like you. Life is diverse and diversity rather than uniformity is the natural state of things. This makes life infinitely interesting. We were created for such an environment. So, the more interesting, diverse, and at times surprising we can make the workplace, the more creative people we will attract.

When outnumbered and facing opposition with much greater resources, surprise can turn disadvantages into advantage. Those who are the best at using surprise are mostly creative types. And one thing that will help foster this is to create a culture of surprise, in your family, business, or organization. More than having surprise birthday parties, this is a culture in which spontaneity is appreciated and used with skill and innovation.

Defending Surprise

In the military, surprise is attacking in unexpected ways, places, or times. In Operation Desert Storm, the biggest surprise of all came from the brilliant new weapons unleashed by U.S. forces, some of which the world had never seen before. "Smart" weapons and GPS navigation gave an overwhelming advantage to the Allies. They used this to take the initiative in the battle and never lost it.

Of course, the biggest surprise was that the U.S. military had devised such weapons, tested them, made them operational, and kept them a secret. This caused a huge initiative among other countries to ramp up spying and create new forms of intelligence gathering, such as computer hacking to steal secrets and plans for future weapons. Some of these were so successful they enabled some countries that were decades behind in technology to catch up quickly. By stealing such information, they also saved themselves the huge number of resources required for research and development.

Today, cyber warfare is a huge part of the strategy and tactics of modern warfare on both offense and defense. Weapons development by adversaries have been set back years by disruptive cyberattacks, such as with Iran's nuclear weapons development.

Likewise, businesses and corporations have been drawn into cyber warfare to protect the development of new products and technologies, or to gain intelligence on the developments of their competitors. Since the surprise of a new product or technology can be a powerful strategy that gives companies advantages over their competitors, using surprise in commerce and defending against it has become a big part of business plans in nearly every major industry.

Surprising Sports

In sports, much time is given to surprise in developing game plans. Whether it's designing a new play that will surprise an opponent or using unexpected personnel in unexpected ways, it has proven to be effective. A well-known example of this was when the 1985 Chicago Bears used the biggest defensive lineman on the team, William "Refrigerator" Perry, to line up as a receiver and catch a touchdown pass in the Super Bowl.

In team sports, a surprise shifting of lineups has often proven to be effective. Teams usually prepare all week for the expected lineup of their opponents. To surprise them with a lineup they are not expecting may only give a team a slight, temporary advantage, but if it's enough to gain the momentum or initiative, it's worth it.

One of the biggest surprises in sports history came in a college basketball championship game between Kansas and North Carolina in 1956. Kansas had the biggest, tallest, and most talented center not only in the country but perhaps ever—the seven-foot plus "Wilt the Stilt" Chamberlain. At the jump ball to begin the game, North Carolina sent out their smallest player who was about two feet shorter than Wilt. The North Carolina coach knew they did not have a player who could outjump Wilt, so why not throw them a surprise? It worked far better than expected. It threw Kansas off their game and North Carolina won in what is still considered one of the greatest games and biggest upsets in college basketball history.

A Divine Surprise

For churches, ministries, and missions, surprise can be a powerful tool for building, mobilizing, and inspiring. The Book of Acts is so full of them it could have been called the "Book of Surprises." Whether it was healing a cripple, blinding a deceiver, or other miracles that captured the attention of whole cities, one could easily believe this is a basic part of the Holy Spirit's nature to release surprises.

To use the strategy of surprise effectively, we must be creative. This should be the special domain of those that know and follow the Creator. How is it that the One who loves diversity so much that He makes every snowflake different and every person unique has a church that is so boringly uniform and predictable? How could any gathering in which the Lord is present be boring? Somewhere there must be a disconnect in that many who claim to be following Him are not.

Creativity is more than just an occasional inspiration, it's a lifestyle. In Scripture, this is called "living water." Water is a good metaphor for creativity because water must be continually flowing and moving to remain pure. If water settles in one place for long, it becomes stagnate. Rivers are going somewhere. It is said you can never step into the same river twice because they are always changing. They are always changing because, at some place, they broke through an obstacle to change direction. So long as a river keeps flowing, relentlessly pursuing, and arriving at its destination, it is changing.

Are we in relentless pursuit of our destination? If so, we too, should be making constant changes to get there.

After all, the way is called the "River of Life." Has there ever been a river that flowed in a completely straight line? Those who follow this River are the most interesting people because they are full of purpose, confident, creative, and full of surprises.

Chapter 8

Economy of Force

JB: Economy of force is the principle of war in which appropriate combat elements are allocated to combat operations against the enemy. Less would be allocated against lower value weaker forces, more would be allocated against stronger and higher value targets. This principle allows commanders to engage an enemy on many fronts while still prioritizing where the main combat power is directed. A less important target or campaign would have a smaller allocation of force than the main target or objective. An entire campaign can be fought as an economy of force operation to fix an enemy in one place and prevent them from reinforcing their own forces at the point of attack.

Battlefield commanders rarely put a maximum level of force into every aspect of an engagement. When trying to employ the principle of mass, a commander must prioritize his objectives. He must determine where the enemy is most vulnerable and where his resources will have the greatest impact.

Once the commander's priorities have been determined, he can then mass his forces to defeat the enemy at a specific time and location called the "main attack." However, enemy threats in other areas cannot be ignored. Therefore, the commander must use a portion of his combat power to confront enemy forces of less priority.

These secondary targets can be important for many reasons. Left unaddressed, these enemy positions could advance and create such a threat that they spoil the main attack. Thus, commanders must apportion some level of effort and combat power to the supporting attacks against less important targets. This is an economy of force operation.

The economy of force principle can also be used to buy time and fix the enemy in a specific location. The objective may not be to fight a decisive engagement with these lesser forces, rather to keep them tied up while the friendly forces mass for the main attack at another point. Economy of force operations include limited attacks, delays, defense, deception, even retrograde or withdrawal operations. The economy of force operation is also frequently used to confuse the enemy as to where the main attack will be.

Special Ops

RJ: All Special Operations units like the Navy SEALs, Delta Force, Air Force Combat Controllers, and Marine Recon were created for economy of force operations. These relatively small units can create the impact of much larger forces at far less cost and risk to friendly forces.

When I (RJ) first met General Jerry Boykin, he confirmed what my studies of the U.S. Army Delta Force had led me to believe. The Delta Force has been recognized as possibly the most effective of all Special Ops forces in the world and is composed of some of the most effective warriors in the world. Yet Delta is made up largely by those who would not have done well in the regular Army. How have so many who may not have been useful in traditional military forces become part of the most extraordinary and effective fighting force in the world? Through the remarkable vision and creativity of some military leaders. The same kind of vision and creativity that took "oddballs" and "misfits" from the corporate world to raise up some of the most successful companies of our day.

To create an effective counterterrorist force like Delta, they had to think far outside the box like the terrorists their mission was to counter. Then they had to develop strategies, tactics, operations, and weapons that were unique to their fight. But these warriors would need to do more than just *think* outside the box—they would need to be comfortable living and fighting there. Those who would be the most comfortable doing this are often those who do not get along well with what most would call the "normal" or "conventional world."

Psychoanalyst R.D. Laing once contended that to be "normal" in this world one had to be insane. He backed this up with both reasoning and studies. It is true that many people who are often rejected because they don't fit into the present system can become some of our most valuable people elsewhere if understood and released to use their unique abilities. Special Operations can do this with extraordinary results.

Still, a force like Delta would not likely do well in conventional warfare, fighting a maneuver battle. We still need conventional thinking and operations. However, in the type of warfare that has emerged in the War on Terror, Special Operations forces like Delta are becoming increasingly important. Blended properly, conventional and Special Operations can make the maximum use of economy of force.

Many former Delta members serve their time in the military and then go on to join local, state, and federal law enforcement as well as private security firms. Along with other veterans of Special Forces they have helped to build a strong counterterrorism presence throughout the world. This has already proven effective and in times ahead could become even more critical. Their seeding of this creative out-of-the-box thinking is helping raise the effectiveness of our national security wherever they go, just as they have helped make the U.S. military one of the largest creative organizations in the world.

Delta Force began when Colonel Charles Beckwith envisioned a special force while serving in Vietnam in the 1960s. He foresaw terrorism becoming a great threat to his country going forward. To combat this, the U.S. needed to build a counterterrorism force. At that time, most of the world had not even heard of "terrorism" or considered it a threat. Beckwith's superiors could not even grasp the concept much less get behind it. But Beckwith had spent a tour with the British Special Air Service (SAS), the legendary WWII commando unit, and knew the U.S. needed similar capabilities to deal with this emerging terrorist threat. Beckwith was relentless in presenting his vision and Delta eventually became a reality.

Trying to cast vision for a type of war that did not yet exist was not easy, especially in an Army steeped in tradition and continually facing budget priorities. After Vietnam, this task became even more difficult. Nevertheless, Delta was born to deal with big, uncommon difficulties and those it faced from the start would become some of the biggest it would ever face. The early Delta Force leaders even used this adversity and resistance as part of their training. This helped create Delta's DNA—the remarkable resilience and resourcefulness that has made it what it is today.

Being considered "a rogue outfit made up of misfits" by most of the Army during its formative years, Delta remained devoted to continually raising their efficiency, capabilities, and resourcefulness to meet any challenge. This was when the U.S. military suffered through some of its lowest morale after the demoralizing defeat of the Vietnam War. Just as we see in Scripture, it is in the darkest times that the greatest leaders and prophets appear. And it was during this time of perhaps the lowest morale in U.S. military history that a remarkable military leadership arose and gave birth to the new Special Ops forces.

The Special Operations units had such an overcoming spirit and commitment to being effective in their mission, it infected the entire military. The U.S. military was transformed from its low state of morale after Vietnam into the most effective and creative fighting force in history as was demonstrated in the astonishing 1991 Gulf War. Never had such weaponry and resourcefulness of fighting men and women been seen on such a level.

Likewise, the best-led companies and organizations advance during difficult times. They may not grow in numbers or sales, but they become more creative, resourceful, and efficient. During difficult times, some of the greatest products and strategies are born because "necessity is the mother of invention."

Great leaders never complain about conditions, they just try to use them. A pro golfer once said, whenever he heard a fellow golfer say he did not like a course, he knew that golfer would not be a threat in that tournament. Great golfers learn to love every course and every challenge as if they were made for them.

Afghanistan

After the 9/11 attacks on the Twin Towers, the U.S. immediately began preparations for offensive operations against the Taliban and Al Qaeda in Afghanistan. The estimated time needed to mobilize and deploy conventional combat forces to defeat these enemies was no less than three months. President George W. Bush and his National Security Team did not want to wait that long to engage those responsible for the attacks against the World Trade Center, so they used Special Forces and Special Ops units to initiate contact with the enemy to learn their strength, disposition, strategies, and tactics. They also wanted to harass and keep them occupied until our main forces were mobilized and in place. Working with local indigenous forces as Force Multipliers, the Special Ops teams on the ground essentially seized most of the cities in Afghanistan before conventional forces could get in the fight. It was a classic economy of force operation.

Small teams of Green Berets infiltrated Afghanistan in late September 2001. Delta and other small Special Ops teams joined forces with the anti-Taliban militias known as the Northern Alliance. Together, they began attacking enemy positions by directing the U.S. Navy and Air Force with devastating effect. This economy of force operation was meant to fix and hold in place Al Qaeda and Taliban forces while U.S. conventional forces mobilized in Uzbekistan. To everyone's surprise, these Special Ops and Special Forces units along with their Afghan allies had taken the entire country before conventional forces could even mobilize.

While this began as an economy of force operation with limited objectives, it became an even greater success than military planners had expected which is often the case. Economy of force operations may not be the main strategy or attack, but they pack a powerful punch often accomplishing far more than expected. This requires commanders to sometimes change their overall strategy to seize these unexpected opportunities.

When Small is Big

History is bursting with examples of small diversionary forces using the economy of force strategy to change the outcome of a conflict. Thus, every economy of force strategy must be planned and carried out with the highest level of commitment and resolve, knowing that such actions can become the main event.

A popular fictional account of how the economy of force strategy can win an entire war is in J.R.R. Tolkien's *The Lord of the Rings* trilogy. Great battles were being waged between good and evil forces, but one little hobbit slipped into the heart of the evil domain and was able to unravel the power of dark forces and bring about their destruction. That was an economy of force action.

Attorney and advisor, Marc Nuttle, may be the person most responsible for bringing down the Iron Curtain yet few people know this. He was sent by President Reagan to help fortify the Ukrainian independence movement. It was so effective Ukraine decided to vote to become independent from the Soviet Union. Soviet leader, Gorbachev, warned that if they voted for independence they would be invaded by the Soviet army. Soviet tanks were sent to mass on the border. Fortified by Marc Nuttle's vision of liberty, the Ukrainians voted for independence even when they expected an immediate invasion from the Soviet Union. The Ukrainians said, just the possibility of their children being free was worth dying for. When Gorbachev did not send in the tanks, it gave Hungary the courage to open their borders to the West. Other Eastern Bloc nations quickly followed and just weeks after the Ukrainian vote for independence, the entire Iron Curtain unraveled.

I call Marc Nuttle "the hobbit." As the great powers of the Cold War were facing off, Marc slipped in and pulled the strings that unraveled the entire Soviet Empire without a single shot being fired. Like Marc, many of history's greatest heroes are unknown to us but they are known in heaven. When the Book of Life is opened, which is God's history book that records the truth of history, we will all be amazed at how many "hobbits" were behind the greatest feats of history.

In fact, it's difficult to be a student of the Bible and not realize this economy of force is one of God's favorite strategies.

Tipping Points

Gladwell's classic book, *The Tipping Point*, is a brilliant study in how small numbers of people can have an impact far beyond expectations. Some of the greatest cultural changes have been accomplished by only a few people—for good or evil. The Marxist Bolsheviks numbered just twenty thousand when they set out to take over Russia, a nation of millions. Likewise, the Nazis were a small fringe group few paid much attention to for years until they suddenly seized power. So, this strategy can be used for or against us.

The most effective strategy ever used to bring about change happened with just twelve men who were taught, trained, empowered, and sent with a message worth dying for. With these twelve, Jesus changed the world more than all conquerors combined. Later, when just two of His wounded followers limped into one of the great cities of the Roman Empire, the officials cried out in terror saying, "Those who have turned the world upside down have now come here to us!" Never underestimate the power of a small, resourceful, determined group.

What matters is the effectiveness of the force, not its size. Less is sometimes more. If only the governments could understand this principle instead of continuing to swell to massive, bureaucratic proportions while accomplishing less and less for the people. The same is true with missions and charities.

An intelligence officer once relayed to me a study which had been done on Christian missions to Haiti and the Dominican Republic. Billions had been poured into Haiti, but only a few hundred million into the Dominican Republic. Yet the results in each were a striking contrast. There was virtually no measurable fruit in Haiti after decades and billions were spent, while there were great results in the Dominican Republic for a fraction of the cost and effort. To explain why, this officer used the example of South Korea after the Korean War.

Compassionate American missions and charities poured resources into South Korea after the war. The intelligence community understood that if this continued the South Korean economy would never restart. Why make shoes if you can go to the mission and get them for free? So, intelligence officers went to the State Department and asked them to help stop this "destructive charity." The State Department listened and agreed to help cut off the flow of free goods to South Korea by well-intentioned but counterproductive missions. When goods were no longer available for free, the South Korean economy kicked into high gear. Soon they had the sixth largest economy in the world and one of the greatest Christian revivals in history.

Likewise, many government and large charity programs have been counterproductive, tragically worsening conditions instead of helping them. Those that receive the most aid are often the ones who remain locked in poverty, just as South Korea would have if some truly smart intelligence officers had not intervened. It is not the fault of those in poverty, so much as the well-meaning but ineffective government social programs that become barriers to progress.

Almost every organization including businesses tend to needlessly swell in size. Then they start majoring in the minors if this is not placed in check. This often happens when departments staff for peak times of demand which often results in being overstaffed the rest of the time. And that is when finding work to keep busy begins to supplant effective and efficient productivity.

This can also become counterproductive to efficiency when a bunch of unnecessary rules and regulations start being developed by those who have nothing better to do. This can become a big burden to organizations, governments, and entire countries.

Leadership promotes what it rewards. When management feels that overseeing many people and a large budget reflects their self-importance, there is no incentive to make the needed cuts or prune for the sake of efficiency. Management efficiency should be measured like a power tool. The efficiency of a power tool is determined by the amount of electricity or fuel needed to produce one horsepower. For example, if it takes one power drill fifty amps to produce one-quarter horsepower and it takes another drill twenty-five amps to produce the same amount of power, the latter is the most efficient.

Economy of force begins with economy, efficiency, and effectiveness as its main purpose. History confirms that 98% of people are ruled by the 2% who are passionate. Having many people may not be as important as having the right people with the right skills and devotion. Better to have a few high impact low maintenance people than to have many low impact high maintenance people.

You never change things by fighting the existing reality. To change something, build a new model that makes the existing model obsolete.

– R. Buckminster Fuller

Chapter 9

Simplicity and Flexibility

Simplicity and flexibility are two principles of war so interconnected we will cover them together.

Simplicity

RJ: In an increasingly complex world, a devotion to keeping policies, procedures, plans, and operations simple is more important than ever. The more parts anything has, the more likely it is to fail. And failure of one part can have a cascading effect on the other parts. The more complex a plan or task is, the more likely it is to have breakdowns. The advantage that complexity can bring makes this a risk worth taking, but we should never add complexity unless it brings a greater advantage than the risks.

The impact of complexity can go further than just creating more breakdowns. Complexity requires a greater mindshare of leaders and managers to plan and oversee and more time and energy to execute. This can not only slow down an operation, but it can also distract from the ability to concentrate, remain aware of unfolding conditions, and cause both threats and opportunities to be missed. This is called "decision fatigue."

The mind can get tired when worked too hard just like the body can. Studies have shown that even top leaders and managers can only make a few high-quality decisions per day. The impact of making too many small decisions can also erode our ability to make big ones. Those who understand this will have others make the less important decisions for them, like what they should eat or wear.

If we train those who work for us to expect we will make every decision for them, they will bring nearly everything to us, sapping our decision-making energy. One way I (RJ) help those on my management team refrain from this is to tell them they can bring to me any problem but with the problem they need to bring a solution. Rarely are any problems brought to me now, because when they work on the solution, they realize what needs to be done and do it.

Some think it's easier to make decisions for others than to let them carry them out, but this is far costlier than we think. Remember the impact we covered in "Unity of Command" about not staying in our lane? Why should we pay someone else if we must do their job? Being a good delegator can be difficult at first, but it's far easier in the long run.

Here is another flawed mentality—the more complex something is the more brilliant. No, real brilliance is when we accomplish something in the most efficient way, at the lowest cost and highest speed.

Simplicity and Flexibility

Simplicity helps keep a force flexible. Those that are flexible can make faster, more agile maneuvers to meet opposing threats and take advantage of opportunities. The same is true with any organization. Without a basic devotion to simplicity, organizations tend to become increasingly complex and bureaucratic which causes them to be less resourceful and less responsive.

Bureaucracies are not only unnecessarily complex organizations, they are also a culture and a mentality that kills creativity and initiative and rewards mediocrity. Bureaucracies are legalistic and overly focused on rules and regulations in place of leadership. Of course, we need some bureaucracy, rules, and regulations but excess kills. And once that becomes ingrained in any culture, it can permeate the rest of the organization or society and ultimately destroy it.

A good example of this is the present dysfunction in the U.S. federal government, which now has six to seven hundred agencies. So many that no one seems to know the exact number. In a cursory study I (RJ) conducted with some knowledgeable government and economic experts, among only a dozen of these agencies we found at least three with no definable purpose. Worse, some seem to exist only to counter the work of other agencies. Hundreds of agencies do nothing but burn through hard-earned tax dollars and create larger deficits.

The constitutional mandate for our federal government was to have two agencies: Defense and Commerce. Do you think we could call this "mission creep?" The point is every organization will trend toward complexity if allowed, which consumes huge resources while accomplishing little to nothing. Isn't that what cancer does? It grows without regard for the rest of the body until it consumes more than the body can give.

Winston Churchill saw growing bureaucracies as one of the largest threats to humanity. At the time, it sounded as ridiculous as any of his other predictions that ultimately came true. Regardless, if the waste these world government bureaucracies now consume were directed toward truly accomplishing something, we could likely stamp out all hunger and poverty on earth. That's another study but this is not just a government problem. Businesses, charities, churches, and ministries of all sizes have this same culture seeping in and consuming huge amounts of energy, focus, and resources.

The Greatest Battle

The battle of bureaucracy is one of the most desperate battles of our time. And the most powerful weapon we have in this fight is simplicity. A good example of how powerful simplicity can be as an action or strategy is Admiral Horatio Nelson's victory in the Battle of Trafalgar.

Some consider the Battle of Trafalgar the most important naval battle of all time. That's debatable but it could easily be in the top two or three. It was a major factor that led to Napoleon's ultimate defeat. Naval battles tend to be very complex but Nelson's battle plan was one of the simplest of all time. In his final meeting with his ship captains on the eve of the battle, he told them they were going to charge into the French fleet. After that, every captain would be free to use his own initiative. He said any captain who had latched his ship to an enemy vessel would be considered to have done their duty, implying their initiative was to fight and not run. But that was the only instruction he gave them.

A major problem in naval battles at that time was communications. Since radios were still a couple of centuries away from being invented, all communications in sea battles were done by signal flags. In naval battles, the sea was usually covered in smoke from the guns, so it could be difficult if not impossible to see flags hoisted from the command ship. Then add to that the typical confusion that comes with most sea battles.

Nelson knew the French captains had been trained to follow orders and not improvise, so he rightly expected this to paralyze them as the battle unfolded. When Nelson's much smaller fleet charged into the French fleet, it brought much enemy confusion and disarray because that was not how naval battles were fought at that time. Nelson's captains used their freedom to create such random attacks, the French never gained the initiative and were soon overwhelmed. Simplicity led to flexibility which made Nelson's fleet more capable of maneuver and nullified the advantage of the French fleet's superior forces.

If we control people to the degree they cannot make mistakes, we will control them to the degree they cannot use their most valuable resources—intelligence, experience, wisdom, and initiative. This is playing not to lose instead of playing to win.

The Deadly Enemy: Complexity

Complexity that leads to inflexibility has not only cost some of the most unnecessary military failures, but also unnecessary loss of lives and loss of empires. In the U.S., it has led to major complications of our future by empowering otherwise weak and easily defeated enemies. How?

Some U.S. presidents have tried to micromanage conflicts from Washington. You can be a great political leader, but foolish and dangerous if you think being good in politics or diplomacy qualifies you to lead armies. This illusion has been very costly to the U.S. in nearly every conflict since World War II.

There are different types of leadership and even great leadership in one field does not guarantee effective leadership in another. What makes one a good politician can also make them a bad military leader and vice versa. High-ranking military leaders who start functioning in political roles require much preparation to be effective in that role. However, few politicians can understand much less be effective in military leadership, especially in today's increasingly complex world. Thus, it takes decades of continual training and experience just to reach flag-officer status in the military.

It is much easier for those in the military to bridge the difference and learn politics. George Washington was a perfect example of this, yet it took George Washington's remarkable wisdom and humility to do this. The transfer of leadership principles from any field to another can be challenging and requires patience, humility, and wisdom. However, those are such rare traits in politicians who presume they can lead anything. This is also a major reason we now have crippling government dysfunction.

In some ways politics can affect a military conflict, but if not kept in the political realm it can have serious consequences. When political considerations are mixed with battle strategy, it can cripple our military at best and destroy it at worst. The President is the Commander-in-Chief for good reason, but that does not mean the President should micromanage strategy, tactics, or operations. Those in the chain of command have been training most of their life for this, and it is still challenging for them. Politicians may have legal authority to intervene in military decisions but that doesn't make it wise.

Killing Our Own

Politically motivated and bureaucratically applied rules of engagement (ROE) have likely caused more U.S. casualties than enemies have in recent wars. Increasingly complex and inflexible ROE not only slow the military's ability to respond to changing battlefield conditions, but some have also been so burdensome and constraining they have made defeating our enemies nearly impossible.

Presidents Johnson and Nixon were both guilty of this in Vietnam, turning what could have been a short, easily winnable war into a long, drawn-out catastrophe. U.S. forces in Vietnam were superior to the enemy in every way by far but were so restricted by ROE it gave the smaller, poorly equipped but flexible enemy forces the advantage. This has come at a great cost in the unnecessary loss of U.S.

lives and resources. And perhaps even more costly has been the loss of respect among our friends and foes, so that even tiny primitive forces now think they can take shots at the U.S. and get away with it and potentially win.

The ROE given to U.S. forces in the Middle East under the Obama Administration required our troops not to fire even on clearly identified enemies unless the enemy fired first! If the enemy gets to fire first, you'll likely be dead and unable to fire back.

Some strikes required chain-of-command approval before being executed. Of course, this gave the enemy time to have a picnic before fading into the darkness. We'll never know how many terrorists got away because of the impossibly complex decision-making apparatus our forces had to endure during this time. Likewise, we may never know how many of our own were killed or wounded because of the impossible ROE.

The restraint on our forces allowed ISIS to grow from a small gang to a powerful caliphate, dominating Syria and Iraq and threatening other nations in the region. When President Trump changed the ROE to give U.S. forces the freedom to do their job, ISIS was quickly eradicated which also put other terrorist organizations on the run.

"Hindsight is 20/20," but perfect hindsight is useless if we don't apply what we learned. Or as General Douglas MacArthur said, "It is fatal to enter any war without the will to win." Far too often this has proven true.

In similar ways, large multinational organizations and businesses have often shackled flexibility and inhibited the initiative of their field managers by trying to micromanage from central headquarters. For large organizations, such extra complications is expensive at best or fatal at worst.

Field commanders or managers may not always make the same decision as headquarters. They will make mistakes, but those mistakes will be far less costly than overmanaging them. The decisions made by those closer to the situation are usually better than those that come from afar.

The Big Advantage

When field commanders or managers are given more trust and authority, it can be a huge morale booster which can have a big impact on operations. When they make the decision, they are naturally more committed to it than when someone else makes the decision. Perhaps it should not be that way, but that is human nature. It is futile to try and deal with people the way they should act instead of the way they do act. Ownership is a huge motivating factor.

Good commanders and managers can be successful but great ones have great victories and great accomplishments. The difference between good and great involves two factors: training and delegation. Those with micromanagement tendencies limit their people as much as those who fail to train them well and training comes more from experience than from lectures.

Remember, "Wisdom comes from experience, and experience comes from mistakes." When we give people the freedom to succeed, we also give them the freedom to fail. The key to overseeing them is to minimize the cost of experience and mistakes while building their confidence and leadership skills which enable them to succeed.

Serious training reflects serious work, and the more serious we are, the more focused and energetic we will become. That's why coaches say they can tell how well their team will play by how good their practices have been. Good morale effects performance and good morale is being relentlessly devoted to the goal.

If we have done our part in training them, our field commanders and managers will be trustworthy and fully capable of handling their responsibilities. We build their confidence and morale even more when they see our trust in them. Likewise, to train and prepare them and then not free them to do their job can also destroy morale.

Chapter 10

Integration of Forces

RJ: Integration of forces in the military has evolved greatly since Clausewitz wrote *On War* in the early 1800s. During the Napoleonic wars, integration of forces meant coordinating the infantry, cavalry, artillery and occasionally the Navy. Now the diversity of forces in an engagement can include units from all branches of the military—different types of aircraft from the Navy, Air Force, Marines, and Army (bombers, fighters, helicopters, drones), airborne and Special Ops forces and different intelligence sources such as the CIA, NSA, and FBI.

All this can make the modern battlefield an extremely complex operation requiring exceptional coordination. If there are forces from other countries involved as allies, the task can be even more daunting. Since Operation Desert Storm in 1991, the U.S. has had plenty of experience with integration of forces within the many continuing conflicts we have been engaged. This has no doubt increased U.S. efficiency in this, but it will likely always be evolving and a major challenge.

Simplicity and Clarity

Efficiency in integration of forces begins with communications. In a multinational force, it's a challenge just to navigate through different languages and customs let alone integrate forces and weapons. To have efficiency in such a complex operation requires a fundamental devotion to the principle of simplicity. Not that it will be simple but kept as simple and free of unnecessary complications as possible.

Understanding the nuances of customs can be critical to communications, which is the basis for all operations. A poignant example of this happened in World War II when a British force came under attack by an overwhelming enemy force. A nearby American commander contacted the British commander to see how they were doing. He replied, "Yes, we're in a bit of a stew here." Not discerning typical British understatement, the American commander thought they were doing fine and went on. The British force was destroyed. It could have been saved by the American force had the communication lines been clearer on either side.

As with any other enterprise, miscommunications have caused many problems in military operations. The name "Babylon" means confusion because the Tower of Babel is where the world's languages were confused. Thus, clear speech may be "freedom from Babylon." Clear speech can also eliminate much confusion in battle and is essential for integration of forces or other groups in any operation.

As daunting as integration may seem, it is necessary. It can be helped by clearly defining terms, signals, or other methods of communication.

I (RJ) was stationed on an aircraft carrier in 1969. The flight deck operations required the coordination of air crews, maintenance crews, ordinance crews, catapult crews, arresting gear crews, fueling operations, and more with only hand signals for communications. Looking down on flight deck operations from the bridge it may have looked like chaos, but it was truly a remarkable level of integration and harmony. This can only occur when everyone knows their job, knows everyone else's job, knows the signals and watches for them.

At a lunch with former NFL Coach Joe Gibbs, I asked him what the most difficult part of his job was as a coach. Without hesitation he said, "Communications." Then he shared stories of how daunting it was to communicate uniformly to the players on the field in all levels of the sport from Pee Wee football to the NFL. To this day, even professional teams are continually trying to improve their communications. In football, miscommunications can cause someone to run the wrong pass route, which often results in interceptions and loss of games. In battle, it can cause someone to bomb their friends. In business, it can cause a loss of customers or a loss of business.

Trained to Listen

The foundation of good communications is the ability to listen. After that, it is having an attention span that doesn't drift. Both are becoming increasingly rare but must be developed in all who are responsible for communications and operations. The military has done a good job with this. Not all their methods are transferable to civilian operations but studying them will help you develop the transferable ones.

In Navy boot camp, I (RJ) was shocked that we spent the first few weeks learning to march. I could not understand how marching could help us in the Navy. I had never seen anyone march on a ship. And since I was going into aviation, I was sure we were not going to march on planes. But then I realized we weren't marching to look good in a parade, we were marching to learn how to listen to instructions and respond in unison.

When first learning to march, if you heard the instructions wrong, you would look stupid going one way while the rest of the company went the other way, but as training progressed the penalty for this increased. Then if you messed up, you did pushups. Later, you ran laps. Then the whole company would have to run laps. If you continued to do this, your company would visit you in the middle of the night for a "blanket party." That was when they threw a blanket over you, and everyone punched you.

Today that might be considered "cruel and unusual punishment," but it sure developed your ability to listen and respond which could later save your life and the lives of many others. Failure of one person to accurately hear instructions has likely cost more lives and unnecessary destruction than most other factors combined that would be cruel and unusual punishment! It's not just about us. In the Navy, not hearing and following instructions could put the entire ship and fleet in jeopardy.

Later, as a professional pilot, I almost daily flew into some of the busiest airports. At times, the airports were so busy the controllers would say they did not have time for us to read back their instructions. If we did not hear our number correctly when it was called or get the headings, altitude, speed, and other instructions right the first time, we could be in big trouble. We had to stay focused as if our life depended on it because it did, along with our passengers, other planes, and people on the ground.

Hearing and following instructions are as important as anything in life or death. Yet having run two organizations that required many people, finding people I could trust to hear instructions was a major challenge. In fact, I have never found anyone good at listening and getting instructions right the first time unless they had been in the military or played a team sport on a high level.

Learning to listen is crucial to integration of force and for life. Even Jesus said, **"Be careful therefore how you listen" (Luke 8:18 AMP).** So, fundamental and crucial to integration is training those who will be a part of it to listen and hear instructions accurately, not translating them through their own inner filter.

Integration Managers

To develop and maintain integration, we need managers who understand the various moving parts of an operation and how they interface to ensure this is done right. Of course, the bigger and more complex the operation the more necessary this becomes. However, more than a few specialists in these points of interface may be necessary as well. If the operation is not large enough to require one full-time person, then at least consider a part-time person or consultant who specializes in integration. Regardless, this must be a part of any operation complex enough to require more than one unit or department.

One example of integration management is airplane design. The team working on designing the wings or landing gear may not know anything about the engines. Such projects require engineers to oversee the interfacing of all the parts, so they fit properly together. You may design brilliant landing gear, but if it doesn't properly attach to the wing or fuselage, what good is it?

Now most engineers you want focused on their specialty. An electrical system engineer may need to know that their system will activate the landing gear and where, but they don't need to understand the hydraulics or other systems any more than is necessary to interface with them. However, you do need some "big-picture" engineers who can oversee the entire project and how it all fits together so they can work out problems and ensure the interfaces work.

In smaller operations, you may not have big-picture people. Instead, you will need to train everyone to understand what people or departments they interface with do, so everyone can be committed to the overall project or operation. Regardless, the interfacing of jobs, departments, or systems must be a priority for every multifaceted organization or department.

Integration can multiply our abilities but doing it poorly can create problems that torpedo the entire project.

Chapter 11

Sustainability

RJ: Sustainability is ensuring the availability of resources for as long as is necessary for the success of the operation.

Not only does this require enough resources, but also the logistics to keep these resources available to the forces when needed. Few battles go as planned, as is true with other operations and projects. Therefore, we must build contingencies and changing dynamics into our plans for sustainability. This often requires supply officers to adjust their logistics.

Napoleon is considered one of the great strategists in military history. Yet his brilliant strategies were often the result of well-designed logistical planning that supplied his troops for sustainability. This created the notorious maneuvering capabilities his enemies could not counter. Napoleon's brilliant troop maneuvers would not have worked without ammunition, food, water, and other needed resources being brilliantly maneuvered as well.

There are several factors that contribute to sustainability. For large, long-term operations, the economy of the country along with its manufacturing and transportation infrastructure is one. Also, weather, geography, roads, rails, and airports near the battlefront can all have major implications for supplying forces and must be considered as part of planned operations.

Companies must consider factors like acquiring the skill force needed to make their products, or the ability to provide a continuous supply of resources and raw materials needed to make them, or transportation of these supplies to the plant and products to the markets. Also, how present, and future economies may affect demand.

Politics and world affairs can also play a major role in sustainability, especially where they affect supply lines or the conversion of plants from domestic to military products. If we can anticipate such changes and make the necessary adjustments, it can mean the difference between a huge win and a colossal failure.

I (RJ) have a friend who is a business professor in one of Europe's top universities. She has said for years the world is making a huge mistake by shipping so much of its manufacturing to Asia. Her contention was, it would soon be far more important to have manufacturing as close to markets as possible, not just where there is cheap labor. She cited several factors that could make transportation of products to markets hazardous. Her theories have been published, widely read, and acknowledged by major industries and governments, yet they all continued doing what she warned them not to do. When Covid-19 hit, it quickly revealed these vulnerabilities to sustain many critical industries.

Even some critical components necessary for military readiness are manufactured in China, which we now know are unreliable friends and partners. This predicament is worth a major study in sustainability and what not to do to achieve it. How we got out of this (presuming we do) will be another great study.

What may look like great and secure supply lines one day may be completely closed the next day. All possible contingencies must be considered while planning for sustainability. Such planning is never a waste of time. In fact, this is often what determines the life or death of any operation. It is that crucial.

Of course, the people force is the main resource needed to accomplish any mission. For churches and missions, the sustainability of a project may be determined by spiritually gifted people and their ability to raise the necessary funds and resources needed for their support. Other disruptive factors may include religious persecution and natural disasters which certain regions are prone to.

Sustainability for any mission, project, or operation must be part of our planning from day one. Or as the wise saying goes, "Hope for the best, but plan for the worst."

Too many historic examples exist of great enterprises failing because they could not be sustained. The armies of the First Crusade failed to reach the Holy Land because they could not forage enough to subsist en route. Instead, to survive they began plundering Christian cities and lands along their route. This not only proved insufficient but also created conflicts between Eastern and Western churches which remain to this day.

More recent examples include Allied forces racing across Europe to capture Nazi Germany then having to wait for their supplies to keep up with them. The Battle of the Bulge was the result of a German attempt to cut off Allied supply lines. This could have not only impeded the Allies successful and speedy advance but nearly also destroyed them.

The truth is, we can become so successful and grow so fast that we stretch our supply lines to the point we become vulnerable to disaster. Had this German attack in December 1944 succeeded, it could have changed the outcome of the entire war, or at least lengthened it. When Eisenhower slowed the Allied advance to prevent them from being overextended, it was not a popular decision but very likely prevented this German attack from succeeding.

As recently as 2003, the main body of American forces racing across Iraq to capture Baghdad were required to slow their pace for logistics to catch up. Evidently, someone learned this lesson from the Battle of the Bulge. Any force in the field, no matter how well equipped and trained, can still fail if it cannot be sustained. Sustainability is an indispensable principle of war without which there can be no success.

We will constantly be facing adversity. There will always be struggles to overcome… If you have a bad attitude, it is because you choose to have one.

– Dale Brown

Don't fear failure. Not failure, but low aim, is the crime. In great attempts it is glorious even to fail.

– Bruce Lee

MSU
MORNINGSTAR UNIVERSITY

COLLEGE OF LEADERSHIP • SCHOOL OF THE PROPHETS • MASTE
COLLEGE OF LEADERSHIP *ONLINE* • ONLINE *SELECT* • ONLINE *L*

MorningStar University is for those seeking to live a high-impact life of unrelenting pur
of the high calling to serve the King of kings with the devotion He deserves.
The greatest leaders are also the greatest followers of Christ, and that is our curriculu
The true Christian life is the greatest adventure we can ever live, and it's also a life of im
like no other. If this is your resolve, MorningStar University may be for you.

FOR MORE INFORMATION VISIT
WWW.MSTARU.COM